SCHOOLING
THE POOR

Critical Studies in Education and Culture Series

Literacy: Reading the Word and the World
Paulo Freire and Donaldo Macedo

The Moral and Spiritual Crisis in Education: A Curriculum for Justice and
Compassion
David Purpel

The Politics of Education: Culture, Power and Liberation
Paulo Freire

Popular Culture, Schooling and the Language of Everyday Life
Henry A. Giroux and Roger I. Simon

Teachers As Intellectuals: Toward a Critical Pedagogy of Learning
Henry A. Giroux

Women Teaching for Change: Gender, Class and Power
Kathleen Weiler

Between Capitalism and Democracy: Educational Policy and the Crisis of the
Welfare State
Svi Shapiro

Critical Psychology and Pedagogy: Interpretation of the Personal World
Edmund Sullivan

Pedagogy and the Struggle for Voice: Issues of Language, Power, and Schooling for
Puerto Ricans
Catherine E. Walsh

Learning Work: A Critical Pedagogy of Work Education
Roger I. Simon, Don Dippo, and Arleen Schenke

Cultural Pedagogy: Art/Education/Politics
David Trend

Raising Curtains on Education: Drama as a Site for Critical Pedagogy
Clar Doyle

Toward a Critical Politics of Teacher Thinking: Mapping the Postmodern
Joe L. Kincheloe

Building Communities of Difference: Higher Education in the Twenty-First Century
William G. Tierney

The Problem of Freedom in Postmodern Education
Tomasz Szkudlarek

Education Still under Siege: Second Edition
Stanley Aronowitz and Henry A. Giroux

STANLEY WILLIAM ROTHSTEIN

SCHOOLING THE POOR

A SOCIAL INQUIRY INTO THE AMERICAN EDUCATIONAL EXPERIENCE

Critical Studies in Education and Culture Series
edited by Henry A. Giroux and Paulo Freire

BERGIN & GARVEY
Westport, Connecticut • London

Library of Congress Cataloging-in-Publication Data

Rothstein, Stanley William
    Schooling the poor : a social inquiry into the American
educational experience / Stanley William Rothstein.
        p.   cm. — (Critical studies in education and culture series,
ISSN 1064–8615)
    Includes bibliographical references and index.
    ISBN 0–89789–372–7
    1. Poor children—Education—United States—History. 2. Charity—
schools—United States—History. 3. Education, Urban—United
States—History. 4. Education—Social aspects—United States—
History. I. Title. II. Series.
LC4091.R68   1994
371.96'7'0973—dc20   93–40161

British Library Cataloguing in Publication Data is available.

Library of Congress Catalog Card Number: 93–40161
ISBN: 0–89789–372–7
ISSN: 1064–8615

First published in 1994

Bergin & Garvey, 88 Post Road West, Westport, CT 06881
An imprint of Greenwood Publishing Group, Inc.

Printed in the United States of America

The paper used in this book complies with the
Permanent Paper Standard issued by the National
Information Standards Organization (Z39.48–1984).
10 9 8 7 6 5 4 3 2 1

For Sue, after 25 years of marriage

One Life — One Love

Contents

Series Foreword

Within the past decade, the debate over defining the meaning and purpose of education has occupied the center of political and social life in the United States. Dominated largely by an aggressive and ongoing attempt by various sectors of the Right, including "fundamentalists," nationalists, and political conservatives, the debate over educational policy has been organized around a set of values and practices that take as their paradigmatic model the laws and ideology of the marketplace and the imperatives of a newly emerging cultural traditionalism.

In the first instance, schooling is being redefined through a corporate ideology that stresses the primacy of choice over community, competition over cooperation, and excellence over equity. At stake here is the imperative to organize public schooling around the related practices of competition, reprivatization, standardization, and individualism.

In the second instance, the New Right has waged a cultural war against schools as part of a wider attempt to contest the emergence of new public cultures and social movements that have begun to demand that schools take seriously the imperatives of living in a multiracial and multicultural democracy. The contours of this cultural offensive are evident in the call by the Right for standardized testing, the rejection of multiculturalism, and the development of curricula around what is euphemistically called a "common culture." In this perspective, the notion of a common culture serves as a referent to denounce any attempt by subordinate groups to challenge the narrow ideological and political parameters by which such a culture both defines and expresses itself. It is not too surprising that the theoretical and political distance between defining schools around a common culture and denouncing cultural difference as the enemy of democratic life is relatively short.

This debate is important not simply because it makes visible the role that schools play as sites of political and cultural contestation but also because it is within this debate that the notion of the United States as an open and democratic society is being questioned and redefined. Moreover, this debate provides a challenge to progressive educators both inside and outside the United States to address a number of conditions central to a postmodern world. First, public schools cannot be seen as either objective or neutral. As institutions actively involved in constructing political subjects and presupposing a vision of the future, they must be dealt with in terms that are simultaneously historical, critical, and transformative. Second, the relationship between knowledge and power in schools places undue emphasis on disciplinary structures and on individual achievement as the primary unit of value. Critical educators need a language that emphasizes how social identities are constructed within unequal relations of power in the schools and how schooling can be organized through interdisciplinary approaches to learning and cultural differences that address the dialectical and multifaceted experiences of everyday life. Third, the existing cultural transformation of U.S. society into a multiracial and multicultural society structured in multiple relations of domination demands that we address how schooling can become sites for cultural democracy rather than channeling colonies reproducing new forms of nativism and racism. Finally, critical educators need a new language that takes seriously the relationship between democracy and the establishment of those teaching and learning conditions that enable forms of self- and social determination in students and teachers. This not only suggests new forms of self-definition for human agency but also points to redistributing power within the school and between the school and the larger society.

Critical Studies in Education and Culture is intended as both a critique and a positive response to these concerns and the debates from which they emerge. Each volume is intended to address the meaning of schooling as a form of cultural politics and cultural work as a pedagogic practice that serves to deepen and extend the possibilities of democratic public life. Broadly conceived, some central considerations present themselves as defining concerns of the series. Within the past decade, a number of new theoretical discourses and vocabularies have emerged that challenge the narrow disciplinary boundaries and theoretical parameters that construct the traditional relationship among knowledge, power, and schooling. The emerging discourses of feminism, postcolonialism, literary studies, cultural studies, and postmodernism have broadened our understanding of how schools work as sites of containment and possibility. No longer content to view schools as objective institutions engaged in the transmission of an unproblematic cultural heritage, the new discourses illuminate how schools function as cultural sites actively engaged in the production of not only knowledge but also social identities. *Critical Studies in Education and Culture* will attempt to encourage this type of analysis by emphasizing how schools might be addressed as border institutions or sites of crossing actively involved in exploring, reworking, and translating the ways in which culture is produced, negotiated, and rewritten.

Emphasizing the centrality of politics, culture, and power, *Critical Studies in Education and Culture* will deal with pedagogic issues that contribute in novel ways to our understanding of how critical knowledge, democratic values, and social practices can provide a basis for teachers, students, and other cultural workers to redefine their roles as engaged and public intellectuals.

As part of a broader attempt to rewrite and refigure the relationship between education and culture, *Critical Studies in Education and Culture* is interested in work that is interdisciplinary and critical and addresses the emergent discourses on gender, race, sexual preference, class, ethnicity, and technology. In this respect, the series is dedicated to opening up new discursive and public spaces for critical interventions into schools and other pedagogic sites. To accomplish this, each volume will attempt to rethink the relationship between language and experience, pedagogy and human agency, and ethics and social responsibility as a part of a larger project for engaging and deepening the prospects of democratic schooling in a multiracial and multicultural society. Concerns central to this series include addressing the political economy and deconstruction of visual, aural, and printed texts, issues of difference and multiculturalism, relationships between language and power, pedagogy as a form of cultural politics, and historical memory and the construction of identity and subjectivity.

Critical Studies in Education and Culture is dedicated to publishing studies that move beyond the boundaries of traditional and existing critical discourses. It is concerned with making public schooling a central expression of democratic culture. In doing so, it emphasizes works that combine cultural politics, pedagogic criticism, and social analyses with self-reflective tactics that challenge and transform those configurations of power that characterize the existing system of education and other public cultures.

Stanley Rothstein's *Schooling the Poor* makes a vital contribution to this series. Rothstein's painstaking analysis appears at a time when the issue of urban education is once again linked dramatically to questions of ethnicity, race, and class. Rothstein performs a theoretical service in reminding us of the historical background that provides a context for understanding the current assault on public schools, especially those schools inhabited by the poor and students of color. In this respect, *Schooling the Poor* provides a historical and theoretical context for rejecting the alleged scientific language and positivistic discourse that fuels the current attempts to undermine the urban public schools while simultaneously policing the students who inhabit them. By focusing on the disciplinary and pedagogic practices that public schools utilized in their attempts to regulate and socialize immigrant and poor students, Rothstein throws an important light on the relationship between the present controversies regarding public schooling and those that erupted in the past. Schools were never innocent, and Rothstein reveals how they have functioned through specific forms of moral and social regulation to discipline, punish, and infantilize in the name of order, national identity, and cultural homogeneity. Class and race are once again on the educational agenda for resurrecting new forms of vocationalization and tracking in the schools, particularly through the attempt either to turn schools over to the logic of the market or to privatize public schooling. Both the underlying assumptions and the practices that inform these attempts have a disreputable legacy in the history of U.S. schooling. It is a legacy that must be revealed so as to not be repeated. Rothstein takes up this task with courage and insight. This is a book that should be read by anyone interested in understanding the historical context that informs the current battle over schooling, national identity, and democracy.

Henry A. Giroux

Preface

From the creation of the first charity associations in the early 1800s, from the opening in New York and Philadelphia of the first Lancastrian schools for pauper boys, and until the 1830s and 1840s, education confined the children of the poor in overcrowded, correction-dominated quasi schools. It restricted pauper boys to enormous classrooms of 300 to 1,000, seeking to order and control their minds and bodies. Through these impersonal pedagogies of surveillance, correction, and confinement, these extraordinary efforts to improve the morals, perceptions, and responses of the poor, the charity schools shaped the understandings and practices of educational institutions in the United States for a century and more.

We must try to imagine, then, those first moments in U.S. history when a righteous people established these first schools for the poor. We must try to describe, from the beginning, those forms of discipline and pedagogy that consigned individualism and learning to one side while glorifying all that was uniform and routine. We want to try to imagine the overworked youngster sitting stiffly at attention on long wooden benches, answering questions mechanically in drafty, unheated rooms, submitting meekly to the schoolmaster in order to avoid the punishments that were routinely meted out to idlers and malcontents.

We must think, too, of the boys who were not in school, whose families would not allow their children to be schooled under the stigma of pauperism. By turns, these charity schools were punitive, and painful, and rote learning of holy scriptures. Also, because the schools were run by teachers and men of the cloth, the entire enterprise was suffused with a righteous, religious aura.

This business of indoctrination and regimentation is an uncomfortable one for schoolteachers. To explore it, we must give up some dearly held myths and ideologies and never let ourselves be persuaded by faulty memories and personal experiences. What we are studying here are the organizational and pedagogic practices that were embraced by Americans as they sought to deal with the increasing problems of crime, poverty, and immigration in the nineteenth and twentieth centuries. What is of interest is the origin and use of penal and militaristic forms of control and their justification by schoolmasters, politicians, and businessmen alike. Thus, we must trace the development from charity schools, with their hundreds of pauper boys in a single classroom, to the common schools and our present, change-resistant public school system. We must study those teacher behaviors that were punitive and used without thought or reflection. Where did they come from, and what were their purposes? Procedures for categorizing individuals, positioning them in assigned sectors, classifying them, requiring them to participate in predetermined processes, instructing their brains and bodies to conform to a previously instituted form, assessing their achievement and registering those appraisals, compelling them to fraternize in public areas where they could be easily noted and controlled were all characteristics of prisons, military encampments, and devout societies of the past. Forcing individuals to answer to the domination of superiors predates modern capitalism. The desire of those in command to produce dutiful, pliable soldiers, disciples, or inmates by constraining their bodily movements had its foundations in antiquity. We shall have to speak of the total denial of individual freedom and the stigma under which the children of the poor received their educational training.

Then, perhaps, we can learn the reasons schools first chose these forms and practices to imitate. Then we can better understand why the schooling of immigrant and urban youth became so different from the ideas that were advocated by John Dewey and other reformers of the nineteenth and twentieth centuries.

In the overcrowded world of nineteenth-century schooling, the children of the immigrant and poor were taught in classrooms of 60 or more. The public delegated to the schoolmaster and, later, to the schoolmarm the authority to control and instruct youngsters in isolated and partitioned locations. The children of the poor spoke only when asked to do so by the teacher. Physical and moral constraint and order were emphasized and conformity highly valued. As for the language of learning, there was little evidence of it, or, rather, there was only the language of correction and regimentation. Urban schools of this period had for their historical models those organizations that were confronted with the problem of controlling, manipulating, and training men who were sometimes armed or otherwise considered as dangerous to themselves or society. Prisons and asylums, especially, were confronted with these problems of organizational order and control. As a rule, such institutions favored geometric and uniform constructions. Buildings and tents were assigned specific locations, and entrances and exits were clearly marked. A negligent or delinquent soldier or inmate could be discovered by simply observing whether his actions or constructions deviated from the prescribed geometric norms. This was the essence of surveillance and regimentation, and it is still used today in many inner city and urban schools and classrooms.

Schooling the Poor is not an attempt to write another history of education but, rather, a social inquiry into the disciplinary and pedagogic practices schooling adopted as it sought to deal with the difficult problems of controlling and socializing the children of the immigrant and poor in our urban centers.

1

Pauper Schools

At the end of the Revolutionary War, education all but disappeared from the United States. In the expanding towns and villages of the new nation, on the frontier and in busy seaports, there was little or no money for formal instruction because of the massive debts incurred during the war with England. For decades afterward, the problem of educating increasing numbers of urban poor and immigrant children would remain a constant and growing concern for the new republic.[1] From the 1790s to the early decades of the next century, tens of thousands of indigents, who had little in the way of formal schooling, scratched out the barest living as unskilled laborers. For centuries past, these unschooled poor had been able to apprentice themselves in guilds, on farms, or as manual laborers. However, from the 1790s onward, the movement from rural to urban settlements caused the poor to expand their presence across the face of the nation.[2] When the Free School Society finally organized itself in 1805, more than 90 percent of the people in the United States had failed to complete a fifth grade education.[3]

There were many who believed that the children of the poor were potential sources of social unrest and crime; urban youth, especially, were seen as noisy, disrespectful, disobedient savages.[4] Moreover, the presence of these poverty-stricken families was a constant rebuke and embarrassment and a living refutation to the conventional wisdom of the day: it was generally assumed that equality of opportunity and industriousness would provide citizens with an improved and improving standard of life, that the pursuance of hard work in a bountiful environment would advance the quality of life for even the poorest of citizens.[5] Also, the poor themselves were seen as a persistent and growing burden on the more affluent citizens of the republic.

From the Revolutionary War to the end of the century, education was not a pressing concern in the United States. According to Ellwood P. Cubberley, there was a steady decline in the number and quality of schools throughout the 13 original states. In any event, around 1786, when religious education was reasserting itself, a Sunday school was organized in Hanover, Virginia, for the children of the city's poor. There were some of these religious schools in other parts of the South: these included a Sunday School for African Children organized in 1787 at Charleston, South Carolina, and the first Sunday schools in Philadelphia. The two largest of these were Katy Ferguson's School for the Poor, opened in New York in 1793, and Samuel Slater's Factory School in 1797 at Pawtucket, Rhode Island. The religious sponsors of these societies in Boston, Philadelphia, and New York had as their stated aim the leveling of class differences in the new urban centers. There were other educational societies scattered about, but at the beginning of the nineteenth century, only five were prominently mentioned: the Evangelical Society of Philadelphia established in 1808, the Female Union for the Promotion of Sabbath Schools (New York) in 1816, the Boston Society for the Moral and Religious Instruction of the Poor in 1816, the Philadelphia Sunday and Adult School Union in 1817, and the American Sunday School Union in 1824. It was a religious duty to educate the children of the indigent and unaffiliated families, and in 1785 the Manumission Society established itself to defend the rights of blacks and to provide them with the rudiments of an elementary education.[6]

The education of the children of pauper families in New York was first addressed by the Association of Women Friends for the Relief of the Poor, which opened the first charity school in 1801. Their schools received aid and encouragement from the state and prospered for many years. In 1823, they were providing free elementary education for 750 children. In 1805, DeWitt Clinton, mayor of New York, accepted the leadership of the newly formed New York Free School Society and promised to subscribe $200 a year for their charity schools for the poor. Some 50 years later, this charity society surrendered its charter and turned over its buildings and equipment to the newly formed public school department of the city, which had been legislated into existence in 1842. The defunct society had educated more than 600,000 children and trained 1,200 teachers during its active lifetime. These educational societies were also active in Baltimore, where the Benevolent Society of the City of Baltimore for the Education of the Female Poor was founded in 1799; a male society was established a year later. Washington, D.C., had free schools that were supported, in part, by the wealthier citizens of that capital in 1804.

Philadelphia had established free societies for training indigent boys in 1800. However, as early as 1810, their schools began to suffer from a lack of adequate funding. In 1806, the Free School Society of New York instituted the first Lancastrian school in which monitors and unpaid assistants were used to control huge classes of pauper boys. By the time of the first Lancastrian school in Philadelphia, funding had become a constant and continuing concern. Lancastrian schools were embraced because of their cost effectiveness; the state of Maryland instituted a system of such schools in 1826. In Mexico, the Lancastrian schools were organized for the state of Texas; they had the virtue of being so low in cost that universal education seemed possible for the first time. According to Thomas Eddy, the initiator of the first free charity school in New York, there was a constant need to find more cost-efficient ways of schooling the increasing numbers of pauper boys.[7] It was for this reason alone that the first Lancastrian schools were greeted so warmly after having been used in England with much success. The society's president, DeWitt Clinton, called the new system a "blessing" and declared that it did for schools what labor-saving devices had done for factories — it made them more efficient and more effective:

When I perceive that many boys . . . have been taught to read and write in two months, who did not know the alphabet, and that even one has accomplished it in three weeks — when I view all the bearings and tendencies of this system — when I behold the extraordinary union of instruction and economy of expense — and when I perceive one great assembly of a thousand children, under the eye of a single teacher, marching with unexampled rapidity and with perfect discipline to the goal of knowledge, I confess that I recognize in Lancaster the benefactor of the human race. I consider his system as creating a new era in education, as a blessing sent down from heaven to redeem the poor and distressed of this world from the power and domination of ignorance.[8]

MORAL SUASION

The success of the New York school caused Philadelphia's Board of Governors to ask Lancaster himself to open a model school in 1818.

Soon, as we have mentioned, Lancastrian schools were in existence in every part of the United States and Mexico, serving the children of the indigent and poor. This strange triumph of authoritarian educational methods had little to do with the better educational results proclaimed by DeWitt Clinton and much to do with the cost-effectiveness of such schools. Also, a new legal requirement forced employers to provide free schooling for their child employees.

Lancastrian schools used older students, unpaid volunteers, and a military arrangement of classroom space to increase the efficiency and order of schooling. Hierarchy was strictly enforced: the teacher sat high above his students on a platform that permitted him to see at a glance what was happening in the classroom. Monitors and assistants scurried back and forth through long lines of pauper boys, giving them orders and maintaining a tight order and control of their bodily movements.

Students were punished for talking, playing, inattention, out of seats; being disobedient or saucy to monitors; snatching books, slates, etc., from each other; moving after the bell rings for silence; stopping to play or making noise in the street on going home from school; staring at persons who may come into the room; blotting or soiling books; having dirty faces or hands; throwing stones; fighting; making a noise before school hours; scratching or cutting the desks.[9]

Lancaster's students attended school as a punishment of birth, seeking to learn correct behavior and moral insights from their betters. They were forced into daily acts of deference and obedience in class-rooms of 365 to 1,000 pupils per teacher; their instruction took place in regimental fashion as young corporals taught them as they stood on assigned spots or sat in long rows of seat benches. The pauper boys were taught reading and catechism at first and, later, subjects of greater difficulty and complexity. Schooling the poor was seen as a Christian duty for the faithful: the pauper boys were predominantly Anglo-Saxons who, with proper training, could be rehabilitated and cured of their social and educational defects.[10]

Of course, these charity schools were born in poverty and poverty was ever their "best excuse for being"; they began to lose much of their popularity after 1830, when their defects were more clearly understood and talk of common, free schools was heard throughout the northern part of the United States. Prior to that time, the military discipline of the Lancastrian schools had been accepted without much thought or reflection. Poor students had taken the role of the unworthy, dependent, subservient person, and we shall see what effects this had in succeeding generations of infant schools and free, state-supported public schools.

The common schools, then, were an extension of the old charity schools, but with this important difference: they sought to provide a common training and curriculum for all. Business favored the development of these common schools, whose founder, Horace Mann, assured them they "would preserve order, extend wealth, and secure property"; in their turn, the business community supported the common schools and their goals.[11] Their values and ideas, which had dominated the economy and cultural life of the new nation, triumphed also in its schools; there was an incorporation, also, of the military practices that distinguished the pauper schools and their Lancastrian variants.

A sequence of dates will serve to orient us: the Pennsylvania Society for the Promotion of Public Economy was founded in 1817, the Pennsylvania Society for the Promotion of Public Schools, an offshoot, was established ten years later. These years were dominated by a struggle to eliminate the old pauper schools and to establish free state schools for all children. It was in 1826 that Josiah Holbrook founded the American Lyceum "to establish on a uniform plan, in every town and village, a society for mutual improvement and the improvement of schools"[12]; in 1831 it was organized into a National Lyceum with this declared purpose: "the advancement of education, especially common schools, and the general diffusion of knowledge." The battle for free state schools had begun in earnest.

THE FREE SCHOOL DEBATES

Throughout this period, and for years afterward, the arguments for and against state-supported common schools preoccupied the thinking of many thoughtful citizens. The end of the pauper schools and the end of the social barriers inherited from an older civilization were central ideas enunciated by the new educational societies. What suffused their reasoning was the belief that such schools were essential in a republican form of government and society. The establishment of such common schools would reduce poverty and crime; it would prevent pauperism and widespread social and economic distress. Also, the religious schools were unable to service the rapidly expanding urban population; the idea of religious schools themselves was questioned as the U.S. culture became more pluralistic. From the formation of charity schools as acts of benevolence and religious duty in the first years of the twentieth century, there was now a shift to a contemptuous evaluation of the pauper schools concept. Schooling under the stigma of pauperism was seen as inimical to the public welfare and a constant offense to the poor; pauper families avoided them when they could, refusing to send their children because of the disgrace attached to them. Education's support was not tied to an increase in worker productivity and citizenship in an urban and increasingly industrial setting. The schooling of U.S. children was a natural right of birth. Ignorance was the enemy of republican government. It was also the enemy of business, which sought more and more skilled and literate workers for its factories, retail outlets, and offices. What free state schools could do best, however, was to assimilate the new immigrants from Ireland and Europe, to establish the new U.S. nation from the diverse populations that were now spreading quickly westward.

Arguments against tax-supported free state schools came from the old aristocrats, the wealthy and conservative elements of the population. What they questioned was the practicality of such schemes. Was it something that could actually be accomplished and sustained? If so, was it right to tax one man's property to pay for the education of another man's child? Would not free state schools make education too common, educating people out of their pauper stations? Was it wise to break down the desirable social barriers that had existed for a millennium and had now taken root in the new land? Was it prudent to abandon the private and parochial schools that had served the nation for a century and more? These were some of the concerns voiced by the opponents of free state schools. They were afraid of the influence of non-English-speaking immigrants, of secular schools, and of government taxation for services most of them would never use.

The arguments became acrimonious and bitter. It was no longer merely a question of free state schools. It was now a struggle to determine the very nature of republican government itself. It was the common people's vision against the anxieties and power of the wealthy and privileged, and it provoked one of the fiercest debates in the new nation's already troubled history.

In their first years, these societies for the furtherance of universal, free schools seemed very impractical indeed. State governments constantly alluded to the problem of funding them, trying first one method and then another. In New England, land endowments, local taxes, and special taxes on parents with children in schools were most prevalent. It is recorded that Connecticut used money from liquor licenses to finance schools as early as 1774; New York ran state lotteries to raise $100,000 for schools in 1799.

However, a profound and fundamental change of attitude began to assert itself after 1825: the direct taxation of all property for the support of common schools became more and more accepted by the U.S. people. "The wealth of the state must educate the children of the state" the slogan went, and it was heard and accepted throughout the free states of the Union.[13] The power of the education societies was strengthened by the new, democratic West, which could not tolerate the notion of pauper schools. Characteristic were the ideas of the Western Academic Institute, founded in 1829 at Cincinnati by Albert Pickett. It proposed that delegations of citizens be sent to state legislatures to demand action on the free state school issue; prominent members such as Samuel Lewis, Lyman Beecher, and Calvin E. Stowe raised money, employed agents to visit existing schools, and tried to elevate the character and quality of schoolteachers in their state. However, the old aristocrats, conservatives, heavy taxpayers, and supporters of church schools still considered the idea of free state schools to be a dangerous one. What bothered them most was their fear that such schools would undermine the family by providing government with too much power to socialize and tax and that they would establish unrealistic expectations in the minds of children of the poorer classes.[14]

From the 1830s to the time of the Civil War, free schools were founded throughout the cities and towns of the United States. Such schools existed in New York as well, even though the state itself did not provide free schooling until 1867! In 1832, when the Lancastrian schools were still very much in existence, New York City provided funding for free schools. There were such schools in Buffalo as early as 1838; Brooklyn followed in 1843. By 1853 the roster of cities providing such schools for their children throughout the north central and southern states was substantial.

In truth, however, the question of free schools was complicated by the rate bill tax on parents of children attending these free schools. A user's fee was charged for services rendered to children. The abolition of this tax in the northern states had to be accomplished before truly free, state-supported schools were a reality. Over a period of years, the rate bill tax was slowly abolished as state aid brought with it supervision and a breakdown of the purely local control of common schools.

Already, Horace Mann had accepted the post of secretary of the state board of education in 1834. When he assumed the position, education was not valued by most Americans, and the post of secretary had low status and pay. However, Horace Mann had an unshakeable faith in the improvability of the human race; he believed that the schools needed to be reformed and made more democratic by including in them people of all classes. He came to his new post with a great deal of enthusiasm, courage, vision, and lofty ideals, and he was a politician with practical legislative experience. Mann realized, first of all, that the schools needed to expand the range of instruction they offered: school organizations and practices were not in harmony with the new social order created by industrialism and urbanization. So, he began to present his views throughout Massachusetts and other nearby states. Soon he had awakened interest and excitement about establishing free common schools that would be more purposeful in their practices and secular in their orientations. Now the struggle to secure common schools began in earnest. The church had always had possession of the education of the young, and the states continued to recognize their dominion in this area by donating land and money for their schools. These endowments stopped about 1800, but grants of state aid for parochial schools continued for the next half century and more. Finally, with the rise of state-supported schools, these church and private educational institutions were taken over and funding provided to them on the same basis as the new state systems.[15]

What the reformers of this period sought were more rational acts of pedagogy and more effective schools for the urban and immigrant poor. Other goals were the development of standards for selecting teachers and administrators and the introduction of new methods of instruction that were more in tune with the needs of the times. Thus, access to professional positions would be denied to the unfit and uniform standards of judgment used to measure the progress of teachers and their students. The new reforms also called for continuous testing of students, more industrial education, setting up infant schools, providing students with guidance, grouping children according to their abilities, and so on.[16] There was a need to standardize and evaluate the progress of students in the face of tens of thousands of immigrant and rural children who were now entering schools in large numbers.

Charity schools disappeared, or almost so; their structures and relationships remained. Often in the same places where schools for pauper boys were housed, the practices of social rejection and penal discipline would be repeated into the twentieth century. Legions of new immigrants from Asia and southeastern Europe would take the part of the ignorant, unworthy student, with results we can still see in our urban schools today. Although new cultures and races would enter the public schools in each generation, pedagogic actions would be the same as they had been in the beginning — essentially a rigorous indoctrination and stratification that socially excluded the children of the poor.

The charity schools, of course, were an aberration borrowed from faraway places. Cost-effectiveness and a desire to socialize and control the increasing numbers of urban and immigrant poor favored the organization of these schools, whose teachers and monitors often serviced hundreds in a single classroom: thus, the constant reports of extremely large classes, ending in the reforms of the 1890s, when school superintendents were trying to bring class sizes below 60 in public schools!

Of all the romantic and mythological histories of schooling in the Massachusetts area and elsewhere, the Lancastrian schools were the only ones that had a great success, for they were able to school large numbers of the poor without costing the state too much money.

A MILITARY DISCIPLINE

Despite this struggle for free, common schools, the criticism of such institutions throughout the nineteenth century had an unchanging theme. In 1880, Charles Francis Adams called school superintendents "drill sergeants," saying their schools resembled cotton mills and prisons more than institutions of learning.[17] When Joseph M. Rice wrote of the schools in the East and Midwest two years later, no one seemed surprised by his charges of extreme student regimentation, no one questioned the accuracy of his observations. Charles W. Eliot of Harvard repeated these same charges about the public schools, deploring "their military or mechanical methods" and their dull uniformity.[18] Among Eliot's reproaches were reports of routine and uninteresting lessons. Schoolmasters, he wrote, accepted a system of norms and discipline that clearly predated the forms of both the charity schools and the common schools that succeeded them. Eliot saw in the rigid status system a training for authoritarian work settings: the strict control of the student's bodily movements, his dependency upon the goodwill of teachers who had absolute authority and control over him, and the social rankings, all mimicked working conditions in the U.S. workplace. These public schools were militaristic, poorly lit, poorly staffed, and poorly heated buildings where the children of the immigrant and poor learned the language and customs of the United States in the most stressful circumstances.[19]

If free schools were linked to so much cultural and class rejection, why did they persist and flourish? Why does the figure of the pompous, self-righteous schoolmaster remain constant throughout the nineteenth century? Why, from the practices inherited from the charity schools, did these militaristic forms of discipline prevail? Perhaps it was because free schooling was supported by all classes of Americans, as Katznelson has pointed out. It calmed a pressing disquiet about rising rates of urban crime and delinquency, carried on ancient traditions of European schooling,[20] and appeared to solve the problem of how to educate and assimilate the multitude of students who continued to emigrate to the United States. In 1890, William Torrey Harris, twice commissioner of education, made his influence felt on the organization and administration of schools. Harris developed the practices of graded schools, schedules, supervision, and selection based on examinations that characterize most public schools today. The custom of keeping attendance records and providing salary schedules for teachers was introduced, and by a series of directives, the authoritarian nature of the public schools was assured. Harris established an educational system in which order and purposeful activity were venerated: the goal was to curtail freedom and aimless behavior, to urge students to greater "effort rather than interest." The schools were prescriptive organizations rather than places where youngsters or teachers could choose their activities and curriculum. They were agencies where routine and regularity were preferred and required, where "silence and industry" were needed to preserve and maintain order and the learning situation.[21]

This same need for order and control was expressed in the social Darwinism that dominated Harris' thinking and the thinking of many of the time: they believed that education had a duty to socialize the animal nature of youth. In public schools throughout the northeastern United States, emphasis on rational self-discipline was the order of the day. The goal was to produce compliant, deferential student-workers who would take their places in the labor market and society when they were older.

A strange philosophy of education for schoolmasters in a democratic culture! However, this was doubtless the sought-after effect of the business community that dominated educational matters then (and now). What they wished to preserve and foster was a society that was basically industrial in its orientations and goals. The schooling of the children of the common folk was seen as a training of productive workers who would also accept the ideas of private property relations without questioning them.

If the student could be removed from his family and from his neighborhood, his training in rational self-discipline could be carried on without interference. His schoolwork and deportment could be observed regularly and graded by teachers; the better students could be identified and separated from those who were less able. At the very moment when critics were castigating the schools for their gloomy, militaristic methods and discipline, the leaders of education were being strongly influenced by business management systems and bureaucratic organizational practices. The decisions of school administrators were often made to improve order in overcrowded institutions, to save money, and to protect jobs. Educational matters were seldom considered, and administrators sought always to "turn out the finest product at the lowest cost."[22]

The notion of common experiences and curriculum, so dear to the hearts of the original common school reformers, was quickly discarded. Because the poor were to do the lesser work of society, their education would have to prepare them accordingly. They were identified at an early age and trained to accept their future places in adult society.

Ungraded schools and classrooms disappeared, or almost so; the concern for individual preferences and needs vanished. A punishment-oriented, authoritarian system with its roots firmly planted in the free school movement of the charity school era remained. The whipping posts of the early schools were gone; schoolmasters no longer carried bundles of switches in their hands. The excess of drill and military command remained, however, along with corporal punishments and other forms of back paddling. Blows with rods, rulers, and the hand were frequently used to impose order. Students were given commands by voice, bells, whistles, and gestures again and again during the school day.[23]

Often, in these public schools, the forms and practices of punishment and control were used without thought or reflection. Where did they come from and what were their first purposes? Methods for distributing people, locating them in confined spatial settings or buildings, sorting them, forcing them to engage in purposeful activity, training their minds and bodies to fit a preconceived mold, evaluating their performances and recording those judgments, forcing them to interact in open spaces where they could be observed and controlled were all features of penal, religious, and military communities centuries earlier.[24] The methods of forcing individuals to respond to commands predate modern organizational forms; the desire of those in authority to create obedient, responsive soldiers, disciples, or inmates by constraining the movement of their bodies had its roots in the prehistory of the human condition.

A DENIAL OF FREEDOM

Thus, we can somewhat understand the curious denial of freedom that distinguished schooling throughout the nineteenth century. We must not, however, minimize the effectiveness of such schools for the new U.S. society. By teaching the immigrant and urban poor children the language and customs of their adopted land, the schools were seen by many as performing an important service. They assured indigenous poor and newcomers that their children would be better able to find employment and acceptance after they completed their educational experiences. The process would make these marginal persons into Americans, molding one people from the diversity of European migrations. Still, education in such schools delivered youngsters into the hands of schoolmasters who were essentially punitive and unaccepting in their attitudes and practices. In the classroom, each child faced the confusing and often cruel experience of being constantly ordered about and judged. Each level of achievement was, potentially, the final one for those who were unsuccessful in their schoolwork. It was because of legal mandates that more and more youngsters were pressed into these overcrowded, state-funded schools. It was out of internal organizational needs and traditions that students were forced to submit to the regimentation and social rejection of their personal backgrounds.[25] The students' experiences were, from their beginnings, a submission to the authority system that held them accountable for their bodily movements and thoughts. They were taught to follow the time constraints of the school's schedules without question or complaint. This was a highly important act of submission, which doubtless alerted parents and students alike to the new realities: training to enter the world of work must, of necessity, be long and arduous.

The words of the English poet of a century earlier were still accepted in spirit by most schoolmasters:

> Students like horses on the road,
> Must be well lashed before they take the load;
> They must be willing for a time to run,
> But you must whip them ere the work be done;
> To tell a boy, that if he will improve,
> His friends will praise him, and his parents love,
> Is doing nothing — he has not a doubt
> But they will love him, nay, applaud without;
> Let no fond sire a boy's ambition trust,
> To make him study, let him learn he must.[26]

Confined in the isolated school building, from which it was increasingly difficult to escape, the student was forced to follow time and movement commands from his teachers. He was a mere automaton in the midst of fellow drudges. He was controlled by adults who observed and assessed his every movement and behavior in the classroom. He was the ignorant one in the learning situation, the subservient one who did not know what he needed to learn or how he should learn it. He was a victim of a docility-utility behavioral model that was misnamed "discipline" by schoolmasters, and the indignities he was forced to endure differed from enslavement only because of cultural understandings and traditions that justified and controlled the behavior of teachers and students alike. The student had his freedom and personal dignity only during those moments when he was outside the school building. Were these the reasons that explained youth's general aversion to schooling and its high levels of truancy? Or was it, rather, the righteousness of schoolmasters that forced students, however passively, to reject those adults who were rejecting them and their familial backgrounds? The schooling experience, with its constant commands, demands, and punishments, these schoolmasters kept assuring everyone, was for the benefit of the children themselves.

Throughout the nineteenth century, and beyond, the protests against this rigid, mechanical training were heard from critics of public education. The superintendent of schools in Rochester, New York, Charles B. Gilbert, wrote that overcrowded urban schools tended to "subordinate the individual." He likened such places to a giant machine that required so much administrative power that they often failed to achieve their intended aims, in this case, educating children.[27] The presence of red tape confused and frustrated the teacher, too. The need to please one's superiors made teachers dependent and unwilling to stray from established and accepted ways of doing things. Gilbert insisted that the factory model was inadequate for public schools. He praised the small, one-room schoolhouse of the rural United States as the place where children were important, where real learning had taken place. Children were being turned into robots, he warned. It was time to smash the machine that was mechanizing our youth. However, the military, penal model of organization persisted, justified as it had always been by its cost-efficiency and the need to control and assimilate the multitudes of potentially unruly, disrespectful youth. What public schools demanded of their schoolmasters was always the same: to discover the methods of discipline and control that would allow them to establish and maintain orderly and safe learning situations. Military precision was needed to move large numbers of youth from one place to another inside the building. The overcrowded schools required punctuality, as did the industrial labor market it sought to serve and preserve. From the confused faces of youngsters in old photographs, we can sense the problem. The children seem to participate in the lessons with only a part of their personalities. They appear to accept their fate, paying attention to the meaningless work without gestures of protest or defiance. The silence of the classroom was a valued control mechanism in schools and in the commercial enterprises that loomed large in the future of these youngsters, who were living through the transition of U.S. society from agrarian to a more industrial economy.

ASSIMILATION

From the beginning, then, the need to socialize and indoctrinate children for their lives in adult society was an important goal of schooling. Youngsters had to be taught the language and values of their country. They had to be taught to accept the private property system as it existed. What was required was the training of youngsters for their use in the factories and offices of the world of work. However, Americanization had to be attended to, also.[28] In 1872, Thomas L. Eliot tried to establish a school system like his father had developed in Saint Louis a generation before him. He sought to found a school organization like the army, in which youth would be trained into a "homogeneous" citizenry and work force who responded in their thoughts, feelings, and actions in the same way. The elements of a graded examination system were borrowed from Boston in an attempt to standardize teaching. This was the beginning of graded classes and strict procedures that brought Western schools "healthy uniformity, hard work, and moral indoctrination" programs that were sorely needed.[29] This training was to be an antidote to the "culture of low imagination and vice" that filled the minds of the young; it was the tide of discipline that would teach students punctuality, order, and industriousness.

A fundamental formalization of educational practices now occurred. The constraint of pauper boys in past generations linked the new common schools to their forms and methods, mimicking penal, military, and religious communities of antiquity. Prison as a form of control and punishment had only recently evolved during the nineteenth century. It appeared to be related to the functioning of the private property system and its glorification of "freedom." The deprivation of a felon's liberty was seen as the most severe aspect of imprisonment, because freedom

was valued above all else in bourgeois society. The role of prisons was
to incarcerate and transform prisoners, to render them docile and useful
citizens. The prison was to be a strict school of discipline in which
corrective training was constantly applied. It was the state institution
that would impose order on convicts so they might be regenerated.[30]
The overcrowded urban schools had the same goals as prisons, but the
intensity of their constraints and punishments was less severe and less
encompassing. They isolated children in classrooms in order to
indoctrinate and instruct their minds and bodies, but they did not do this
24 hours a day. The new schools in the West taught youngsters to be
good soldiers, to respond to coercion submissively. The unfortunate students sat in bare classrooms and listened in silence, often while teachers
ridiculed them and their backgrounds. During this period, the image of
the ignorant and unworthy student became permanently fixed in the
schoolmaster's mind.[31] What upset the teacher's serenity was not the
stupidity of his pupils, but their laziness. They were disinterested and
unwilling or unable to enter into classroom work with their full energies
and capabilities. In the oppressive classrooms of public schools, students
were confronted by teachers whose personalities expanded as they
taught their predigested facts; intense smiles shone from their counte-
nances, the deep commitment clearly evident. An anxious, disinterested
class of youngsters tried to draw back from this unequal encounter, so
resembling the relationships between workers and their employers. They
sought to preserve whatever parts of their self-respect and dignity they
could salvage in these difficult circumstances. Of course it was precisely
this tug of war between demanding, willful teachers and passive pupils
that was at the core of the problems between them. They were separated
from one another by a rigid status system and the power teachers had to
affect the lives of their students. Both were isolated by invisible barriers
neither could surmount. The teachers no longer saw children who
needed to learn about the world in which they lived. The students saw
only rigid taskmasters who had great power over their lives while they
were in school. It was the charity schools reborn. All the condescension,
all the fear of the poor and immigrant youngsters, all the need to control
them — all these old anxieties seemed to reappear again and again
during the latter half of the nineteenth century.[32]

However, if education was linked in the public mind with so many
features of penal and inmate systems, why did the schools persist and
expand? Certainly urban schools were consummate examples of moral
and institutional suasion, attempting to constrain the mind and bodies of
students at every turn. Why did the language of education bespeak of

learning, instruction, and individual development while daily practices were so obsessed with organizational themes? Partly it was because it was meant to mask the struggle between teachers and students, between the aspirations of the immigrant and urban poor and the schools' mandate to reproduce U.S. society. Partly, too, it was because the schools were serving as entry to the economic sector, and that sector was essentially autocratic and undemocratic in nature. It needed and demanded docile, subservient, and useful workers for its labor force.

PURPOSEFUL ACTIVITY

What, then, was this fascination with penal discipline and military forms of organization?

First, discipline in overcrowded schools was always exercised in the name of the common organizational goals. The rules and regulations were used to train children from different backgrounds in predetermined, uniformed styles. This was what was often called "regimentation" by schooling's critics. The organization's control practices sought to eliminate confusion, aimless movements, and emotionalism while commending coordination and purposeful activity. It sought to create uniform behavior and work patterns. Students were seen as objects or parts of a larger social system who had to be controlled and moved about for their own good and the common safety.

Second, these rules and regulations were part of a power structure that was dependent upon legal-rational authority.[33] Every member of the teaching staff had been licensed by the state to perform his or her work in the schools. This system had a great deal of success because of its inherent simplicity. It gave schoolteachers certain rights and responsibilities within a rigidly defined status system and allowed for the use of arbitrary pedagogic practices. Inside the building, teachers were in control; they were the ones who judged students by testing them, observing, and standardizing the modalities by which student behavior and work could be evaluated.

Finally, the overcrowded schools of the last part of the nineteenth century had for their historical model the military organization, for example, that establishment that was confronted with the problem of controlling, manipulating, and training large numbers of men who were armed and presumed to be dangerous. Prisons and asylums also were confronted with similar organizational problems. Such places glorified geometric and uniform formations and constructions. Buildings and tents were assigned specific locations, entrances, and exits. A malfunctioning soldier could be discovered by an officer simply by observing whether his tent deviated from the prescribed geometric norms. This was the essence of surveillance and regimentation in human affairs.

The construction of urban schools during this period also provided an example of the constraining nature of such establishments. Classrooms, auditoriums, hallways, and other areas were built so that teachers could see and judge the behavior of students at every moment of the day. Confinement, perhaps the oldest form of discipline, was replaced by communal living and performed in open spaces where students could be easily observed and corrected. Classrooms were located along hallways that were uniformly distant from one another and visible through windows in their doors. Students were almost always in the presence of teachers and confined to assigned locations inside classrooms. In lunchrooms, tables were often placed so movements of pupils could be inspected at a glance; tables were dismissed in order, and loiterers were easily identified. In the lavatories, there were often half doors or no doors at all. Privacy was conspicuously absent in these overcrowded, poorly lit, poorly heated buildings.

The public school was structured to provide training for the children of the common people. It was to provide a better example of proper deportment and industry, thereby assuring U.S. society disciplined workers and citizens. The texts, workbooks, and predigested learning experiences ware simply another form of regimentation and indoctrination.[34] No longer was the school merely the place where religion or numbers and letters were taught; now it was a place where students were forced to submit to rationalized schoolwork and daily routines that prepared them for work in the machine society of the times.

The public school of the nineteenth century, then, was first and foremost a training and retention center for immigrant and urban youth. Ideally, its discipline would allow a teacher to see and evaluate everything that was happening in the classroom at a glance. Circular buildings, with their doorways facing inward, had helped prisons and penal institutions achieve this goal of constant surveillance and control. Administrators were placed so they could see, check, and constrain the actions of inmates or convicts at every moment during the day or night.[35] All communications and directives were handed down the administrative hierarchy or control structure, and all activities were monitored and evaluated by staff members.

Of course, the very size of the urban schools made it impossible for school administrators to see and hear everything that was going on in the school. This made it necessary for another authority figure to convey the needed information to the building's supervisor or principal. There was a need for assistants who could perform the surveillance and evaluation functions within the enclosed classrooms themselves. This meant that a hierarchial structure had to be put in place and sustained; teachers had to assume the discipline tasks in order to insure the constant surveillance of the students under their control. Their primary task became one of emphasizing schoolwork and deportment while keeping students busy and under constant scrutiny.

The essential features of discipline that developed in these schools included the following characteristics: (1) Discipline was concerned with moving students around within the confined spaces of the building and according to the daily schedule. In the overcrowded schools of an increasingly urbanized society, it required the student's enclosure in a distinct, walled community. Therein, the coercive nature of the discipline could be carried through without interference from parents or outsiders. There the students, that collection of rowdies from diverse backgrounds and cultures, had to be put in their place from the start; fighting and disorderly conduct had to be prohibited; the peace and serenity of the surrounding community had to be preserved and the fears of merchants and residents calmed. Truancy had to be prevented or punished and the costs of education tightly controlled. The school had to be carefully bounded, thereby helping teachers to maintain order within its confines.

The rapidly growing factories, bureaucracies, and armies of the late nineteenth century needed a certain type of citizen-worker, one akin to those who had lived in the communal societies of the precapitalist period. The goal was to minimize interruptions and disturbances so that production could be greatly increased, so that the language and culture could be taught to the children of immigrants and the urban poor.

(2) Disciplinary needs, however, evolved from the conditions of enclosed spaces in emerging urban schools. It depended upon separation and partitioning routines to achieve social order. Each student had his own classroom and seat, and each classroom had its own assigned students. Uniformity had to be a complete as possible, with students being forced to "toe the crack" or line on the floor when reciting for the teacher.[36] Students could not be permitted to wander aimlessly through the halls or classrooms; they could not be allowed to absent themselves from scheduled classes or events. Everything had to be done to force them to concentrate, to attend to the arbitrary schoolwork, to obey the authority of the classroom teacher. In this way, students were either

present or absent from their assigned places and teachers could locate them inside the building at any time of the school day. Also, lessons could be planned, meetings held, and supervision conducted in a prescribed manner. To assess, to judge, to record, and to calculate the merits of individual students in the school: that was and is the goal that disciplinary systems sought to achieve and maintain. All this was done to facilitate the work of those who were working in the school: the teachers, representatives of the adult society, needed orderly and controlled environments if they were to do their work properly. The use and analysis of space was part of this discipline system that kept students from straying from the path of purposeful behavior.

(3) Functional sites were established inside the building. Certain areas were left to the discretion of the teachers and administrators. Spaces where supervision could take place, where disciplinary interviews could happen, where the sick could be isolated and ministered to — even these areas employed surveillance methods to control the students who congregated there. The legitimate teaching of knowledge and deportment was merely a part of the larger control process; the control over the bodily movements of students who might otherwise quit school or seek to continue their training elsewhere was also supported by common custom and state law.

(4) Discipline, especially in the schools of the latter part of the nineteenth century, was defined by an individual's right to be present in a specific location at a particular time. A person's status was of the utmost importance in determining what role he or she played in the normal give and take of school life. Discipline was merely one way that rank and privilege were affirmed inside the building itself. It designated the authority of different persons and groups as they conducted their business of public instruction. In earlier periods, rank was shown by an individual's seat in a particular row and file, by a class position, or by a placard placed in the corridors, schoolyards, or assembly rooms. Also, examinations were used to rank students, following the example of the Boston schools of the 1860s and 1870s, and this was done throughout a student's career. Age, too, was used to evaluate performance and behavior in competitive situations.

By assigning places to students, the routinization and regimentation of schoolwork became possible — teacher supervision became a simple matter of noticing whether students were deviating from the prescribed norms and demands of the teacher. Rewards and punishments also were facilitated by this surveillance system. Some educators even hoped to establish classrooms in which a pupil's ability, character, diligence, deportment, and status were distinguished by his or her seat and row placement.

The charity schools of the early part of the century had given inner discipline and correct moral thinking a high place in their goals and objectives. Beginning with the classical period and earlier, it was customary for schooling to be molded by the needs and understandings of a particular society. In ancient Sparta, education had been shaped by the need of the embattled nation to produce soldiers who would devote their lives willingly to the rough life of the encampment: values such as loyalty and kinship, simplicity and physical strength, abstinence and animalism, lust and perseverence were highly regarded.[37] In Athenian schools, education sought to bring the finer nature of man to the surface, providing students from upper-class families with a deeper appreciation of the arts, sciences, and philosophies of life. The one common denominator was the desire of every social system to recreate itself, to produce future citizens who would carry on the ideals and values of the existing order. In U.S. public schools during the nineteenth century, the children were seen as the raw materials that had to be transformed into dependable, efficient workers who would perform routine, uninteresting work in the factories and commercial offices of industrial society. This explains, in part, the constant demand for standardization, predigested lessons and learning materials, and the physical arrangements of the buildings and classrooms; they facilitated surveillance and evaluation by a relatively few teachers and administrators. Purposeful movements and activities were encouraged, as they were in the industrial workplaces that were developing in the United States at that time.

Strangely, this simulation of the autocratic workplaces had unintended effects for teachers and students alike. Personal relationships became so charged with resentments and repressed emotions that the schools often failed to accomplish their intended goals. Teaching was no longer merely the transmission and rote recitation of arbitrary and uninteresting materials; the grading and selection of successful and unsuccessful students became an important end in itself, stifling classroom communication. Between teachers and students, an unbridgeable gulf developed. It was necessary to coerce students to be neat, punctual, and attentive to meaningless lessons. Observers bore witness to regimentation's ugly outcomes: teachers became little more than martinets and drillmasters; children became less human and more robotized in their responses. The work of the students was often boring and incomprehensible to them. Their deportment was more suitable for the military encampment than the school. Obeying the commands of teachers without question was the standard sought, and yet, it had the unintended effect of subverting thinking and inquiry, two supposed goals of enlightened education. Students took their places silently and sat through the lessons without involving themselves or questioning any of the materials presented to them. Witness the impassive faces in old photographs showing youngsters sitting attentively in seats that are firmly bolted to the floor. Witness also the shocking reports of Cubberley after his visits to the Portland, Oregon, schools in the early twentieth century. A look of passiveness haunts these faces of the young: the arduous experience of schooling had already taught them to expect the worst in their dealings with teachers. The head of the child was held back, the better to see and hear what was being said by the constantly talking teacher; the hands were clasped so they could be more easily observed; and the back was ramrod straight. This posture of the student was akin to that of a robot or a soldier during inspection![38]

Soon these organizational practices were influencing architectural forms. Buildings were larger and constructed of steel and concrete, like many of the new businesses of this period. Heating and ventilation were installed so that large numbers of students could be better served inside the building; modern toilet facilities were also provided.

Educators found in these physical structures a means of assimilating the diverse cultural and linguistic characteristics of immigrant populations. The legions of youth also seemed to want this transformation of the self! And, at the end of the nineteenth century, the need seemed more apparent than ever. It was hoped that a common educational experience and a unifying training would make the newcomers and those from marginal families loyal and productive citizens of the republic. Being required to serve hundreds of thousands of children in overcrowded urban schools caused educators to embrace, more and more, the ideas of scientific management that were then coming into vogue. Bureaucracy was accepted as a reasonable way of simplifying tasks and routinizing school life after the work of William Torrey Harris, and it was in these new organizational environments that public education attempted to reproduce the conditions of its own existence and that of the emerging industrial system.

Bureaucracy was embraced because, as with the Lancastrian schools at the beginning of the century, it was the most efficient and least costly way to organize the schooling of the poor and common folk. It was efficient, first, because the rules and regulations made it possible to judge who was doing what they were supposed to do and who was not. Students' failure to conform was easily observed and uniformly punished. Youngsters knew what they could expect if they engaged in undisciplined, deviant behaviors. Although theorists were seeking new forms of organization, most educators of this period accepted the military bureaucracy model and taught by recitation and rote, drilling students routinely and observing and evaluating their every movement inside the classroom or building. Authoritarianism was the standard, as it had been throughout recorded history, with almost no exceptions, but now it had legal-rational authority to support its right to arbitrary rule inside the school buildings.

What did they herald, then, these schools of continuous observation and control? Certainly, because they were obsessed with the control of large numbers of students in limited spatial areas, they presaged a school system of coercion and comparative evaluations. Continuous judgments followed by rewards and punishments were the norm, and order was given the highest priority. The urban schools set out to transform the personalities and cultural backgrounds of the students, seeking to produce docile, utilitarian citizens and workers who would accept the rationalized work processes and social relations of industrial society. This was the important function they had to accomplish. Schools had to provide the ever-expanding industrial and commercial industries with the rationalized individual who would not shun or push aside the meaningless tasks of such organizations.

We conclude this overview with an observation: education in the nineteenth century was one of the most expensive and important operations of state governments. Its features were fixed by concerns for crime-control measures and the need to assimilate increasing numbers of urban poor and immigrant youth into the ever-expanding U.S. system. However, certain practices and ideas appeared again and again. Moral training of students was prominently mentioned in the charity schools and the common schools that followed them. Later the theme emerged in the public schools of the Midwest and Far West and in those systems that served immigrants from eastern and southern Europe. The attitudes of condescension and rejection toward pauper children and the later immigrant and urban poor students was a constant, even though it went against the stated goals of the system. In organizational practices, there was little to choose from between the charity schools for pauper boys and these first, faltering steps toward free, universal schooling for all. The schools owed their rigid punishment practices to coercive organizations of the distant past.

Education, with its peculiar need to control and manipulate the mind and body of the urban poor and immigrant learner, found it convenient to adopt variations on these ancient forms of compulsion.

Building upon the military efficiency of the first Lancastrian schools was a newer authoritarian organizational structure: legal-rational bureaucracy. However, it was not the idealized model with which teachers identified themselves in the end. The noble ideas of the common school reformers were subverted by the needs of overcrowded schools for the children of the common folk. Educators, then, inherited more than just the buildings and teachers from the old Lancastrian school system — they inherited the old resentments toward the weak and poor. Empowered in the schools, they were envied; punishing, they were feared; with the preferred language and culture of the school at their command, they were spurned by the students they were supposed to enlighten. Such consequences were more than the founders of the free, common schools movement could have predicted. Such had become the paradox of educating the children of the immigrant and poor at the end of the nineteenth century. Even in its most enlightened forms, these schools isolated students from their teachers. They became, in the childhood of every citizen, the most difficult training imaginable. Schools forced children to compete endlessly for a distant prize that was beyond their understanding or ken. To renounce schooling was to meet with the full disapproval and punishment of the legal system and the entire social order.

To the world of these overcrowded schools, also, belonged to the "proper-punishment-for-infractions" syndrome.[39] In classrooms, however, it had this difference: the punishments teachers meted out were done in the name of enlightening the students to their future possibilities. The justification for schooling's practices were that they improved the mind of the student by teaching him respect for the time and property of others.

Thus, schooling was no longer simply a matter of instruction, in the literal sense of that word. It had other social functions that had to be accomplished. It was not concerned with what a student learned but with when and how he learned it. Through examinations and observations, a process of social and educational selection helped teachers and administrators to identify high achievers from lower ones. When students had completed their schooling, they received credentials that further identified and delimited their opportunities in the world of work. Education was forced into the business of indoctrinating students in order to assimilate immigrants and the urban poor into the mainstream of society. This indoctrination was one of schooling's most important functions in the nineteenth century.

To summarize, many of the organizational forms and practices of public schools were in existence in the 1800s and earlier. The pressing concerns associated with schooling pauper children, the high costs of educating the children of the common folk had lost none of their immediacy in the twentieth century. Structures persisted, now obvious, now less so, forming rigid practices that shaped the ever-larger urban school districts. Education continued to be an onerous, unpleasant experience for most youngsters; the inflexible routines and punishment syndromes survived in spite of the changes wrought by new generations of students and technological revolutions. Authoritarianism continued to dominate the organizational practices of urban schools. Education could no longer resist or deny the demands of overcrowded, impersonal institutions; it could not escape from its past history and culture as long as the individual student was denied his worth and capabilities and submerged in an impersonal organizational ethos in order to improve the efficiency of indoctrination efforts and the cost-efficiency of the system.

NOTES

1. Stanley K. Schultz, *The Culture Factory: Boston Public Schools 1789–1860.* (New York: Oxford University Press, 1973), pp. 261–63; see also Lawrence A. Cremin, *Traditions of American Education* (New York: Vintage Books, 1964), pp. 33–37; and Carl E. Kaestle and Maris A. Vonovskis, *Education and Social Change in Nineteenth Century Massachusetts* (Cambridge: Cambridge University Press, 1980).

2. David Rothman, *Discovery of the Asylum* (Boston, Mass.: Little, Brown, 1971), pp. 14–15.

3. Schultz, *The Culture Factory*, pp. 243–46; see also Ira Katznelson and Margaret Weir, *Schooling for All: Class, Race, and the Decline of the Democratic Ideal* (New York: Basic Books, 1985), pp. 3–18.

4. Franklin Trollope, *Domestic Manners of Americans* (New York: Knopf, 1949), pp. 212–13; see also Basil Bernstein, *Theoretical Studies Towards a Sociology of Language, Volume 1, Class, Codes, and Control* (London: Routledge & Kegan Paul, 1975), pp. 121–23.

5. Robert Berthoff, *An Unsettled People: Social Order and Disorder in American History* (New York: Harper & Row, 1971), pp. 212–13; see also David Tyack, *The One Best System: A History of American Urban Education* (Cambridge, Mass.: Harvard University Press, 1974), pp. 9–10.

6. Ellwood P. Cubberley, *Public Education in the United States* (Cambridge, Mass.: Houghton-Mifflin, 1963), pp. 120–36.

7. Nathan Edwards and Horace G. Richey, *The School in the American Social Order* (Boston, Mass.: Houghton-Mifflin, 1963), pp. 237–38.

8. Cubberley, *Public Education in the United States* pp. 133–34.

9. David Nasaw, *Schooled to Order* (New York: Oxford University Press, 1979), pp. 20–21.

10. Lawrence A. Cremin, *The Transformation of the School: Progressivism in American Education* (New York: Random House, Vintage Books, 1964), pp. 25–31.

11. Nasaw, *Schooled to Order*, p. 80.

12. Horace Mann, "Twelfth Annual Report of the Secretary of the Board (1848)," in *The Republic and the School: Horace Mann on the Education of Free Men*, ed. Lawrence Cremin (New York: Teachers College Press, 1957), pp. 100–1.

13. Ellwood P. Cubberley, *The History of Education* (Cambridge, Mass.: Houghton-Mifflin, 1920), pp. 671–72.

14. Cubberley, *Public Education in the United States*, pp. 163–211.

15. Ibid., pp. 189–98; see also Michael B. Katz, *The Irony of School Reform* (Cambridge, Mass.: Harvard University Press, 1968).

16. Cubberley, *Public Education in the United States*, pp. 137–41; see also Michael B. Katz, "The New Departure in Quincy, 1873–1881," in *Education in American History*, ed. Michael B. Katz (New York: Praeger, 1973), pp. 68–71.

17. Katz, *Education in American History*, pp. 80–82.

18. Ibid., p. 84.

19. Cremin, *The Transformation of the School*, pp. 3–8.

20. Cubberley, *The History of Education*, pp. 633–640; see also Hannah B. Clark, *The Public Schools in Chicago* (Chicago, Ill.: University of Chicago Press, 1897).

21. Robert C. Hummel and John M. Nagle, *Urban Education in America* (New York: Oxford University Press, 1973), pp. 31–35.

22. Cubberley, *Public Education in the United States*, pp. 126–37.

23. Ibid., pp. 322, 328.

24. Michel Foucault, *Discipline and Punishment: The Birth of the Prison* (New York: Pantheon Books, 1977), pp. 231–33.

25. Erving Goffman, *Asylums: Essays on the Social Situation of Mental Patients and Other Inmates* (New York: Anchor Books, Doubleday & Company, 1961), pp. 125–55.

26. Cubberley, *The History of Education*, p. 456.

27. David Tyack, "Bureaucracy and the Common School: The Example of Portland, Oregon 1851–1913," in *Education in American History*, ed. Katz, pp. 167–68.

28. Ibid., pp. 168–69.

29. Ibid., pp. 172–74.

30. Foucault, *Discipline and Punishment*, pp. 232–33.

31. Cubberley, *Public Education in the United States*, p. 383.

32. Tyack, "Bureaucracy and the Common School," p. 169; see also Willard Waller, *The Sociology of Teaching* (New York: Russell & Russell, 1932).

33. Max Weber, "The Essential of Bureaucratic Organization: An Ideal Type of Construction," in *Theory of Social and Economic Organization*, ed. Talcott Parsons (New York: Oxford University Press, 1947), p. 242.

34. Stanley Rothstein, "Orientations: First Impressions in an Urban Junior High School," *Urban Education* 14 (April 1979): 91–116; see also Stanley W. Rothstein, *Identity and Ideology: Sociocultural Theories of Schooling* (New York: Greenwood Press, 1991), pp. 109–13.

35. Foucault, *Discipline and Punishment*, pp. 169–79.

36. Cubberley, *Public Education in the United States*, p. 322.

37. See Emile Durkheim, *Education and Sociology* (Glencoe, Ill.: Free Press, 1956), for needs of societies and educational systems.

38. Tyack, "Bureaucracy and the Common School," p. 164.

39. Foucault, *Discipline and Punishment*, p. 157.

2

Houses of Confinement

During the last half of the nineteenth century, compulsory attendance laws were enacted throughout the United States and its territories. In the expanding urban centers and on the frontier, there now lived many immigrant families who did not possess the language or cultural background of their adopted homeland. For decades, they had managed without schooling of any kind. Now, the demands of a technological and bureaucratic society brought the matter of compulsion and confinement to the forefront of U.S. thought:

The principle of compulsory education is steadily gaining ground. Steps in advance are being taken here and there all the time. Since 1886 no less than 16 states and territories have made their former laws more stringent. The arguments and discussions of thirty years or more have been gradually crystallizing in the direction of requiring by law all parents to provide a minimum of school instruction for their children. This tendency is unmistakable.[1]

This commitment to compulsory education had European origins. It was based upon the ideas of the Protestant Reformation and its belief that education was an important path to salvation. Luther had supported strongly the notion that education should be made available to all, that the state should make it available and constrain its citizens to partake of it.[2] The Lutheran and Calvinist traditions both had as their core belief the idea that the faithful needed an education that would allow them to read the Bible. In 1619 the Duchy of Weimar instituted compulsory schooling for children from the ages of 6 to 12; in 1642 Duke Ernest did the same in Gotha. In Holland, the Synod of Dort (1618) tried to implement compulsory attendance, and in 1646 the Scotch Parliament ordered the compulsory establishment of schools.

Thereafter, an entire network of compulsory education spread across the German provinces and states. King Frederick William I, in 1717, undertook to provide such schooling for all of his citizens, saying that "hereafter wherever there are schools in the place the parents shall be obliged, under severe penalties, to send their children to school . . . daily in the winter, but in the summer at least twice a week." Financing for such schools was to be provided by community funds. By 1794 these laws had been codified so that "instruction in school must be continued until the child is found to possess the knowledge necessary to every rational being." This is proof that even at this early time, a certain significance was attached to the socializing powers of schooling: that which had been thrust upon the stage of history as a religious requirement of conscience was not being used by secular powers to pacify and unite their citizens. In little over a century, compulsory education had become the norm for the more advanced nations of central and northern Europe.

In 1642 the Massachusetts General Court ordered selectmen to observe whether parents and apprentice masters were preparing youngsters "to read and understand the principles of religion and the capital laws of the country."[3] They also sought to learn whether youngsters were being trained "in learning and labor." This was the first instance of a legislative body in the English-speaking world ordering that all children should be taught to read. In 1647 the Massachusetts Court ordered the establishment of schools so that compulsory attendance could be more easily enforced, providing the foundations upon which the free school movement modeled itself a century later. Still, compulsory education never took hold in the Anglican colonies of the New World and in England. The act of compulsion conferred upon schooling a governmental and social sanction that provided a haven for institutional learning. It organized the world into a coherent unity that ethically judged and evaluated the social conditions of teachers and students alike. Perhaps it was a reaction to confinement in state institutions and the loss of liberty that caused the United States not to pursue compulsory education during the seventeenth and eighteenth centuries. Later, these themes of liberation through knowledge were present during the French Revolution, when compulsory education was ordered for all citizens in 1792; this gave lip service to an idea that was rendered meaningless by the Napoleonic Wars. France did not embrace compulsory education until 1882; England did not provide comprehensive laws until the twentieth century.[4]

Compulsory education, that social movement that spanned three centuries, was a legal response to the twin scourges of urbanism and industrialism: legal, in the precise sense that the emerging legal-rational era gave to it — the structuring of learning so that individuals could be more easily fitted into the emerging machine culture.[5] The authority of the public schools was based on their role as the educational agency of the state, the institution that transformed immigrant and urban poor children into productive workers and citizens. The school was accepted by all classes of people because it congregated children in a professional setting and rendered them obedient and harmless. Schools were like a well-disciplined workplace, a military encampment, a detention center; yet, the intensity of their coerciveness had a different intensity. Their authority was based upon the legal mandates of the state and the common sense understandings of the people. These made the schools seem like the natural places for civilizing the savage natures of youth. It gave them the responsibilities for reproducing the conditions and beliefs of U.S. society. The compulsory attendance laws came after free state schools were founded in the United States; they were a legal demand for attendance so that the corrective pedagogies of public education could be performed on children and they could be prepared for the rigors of adult life in the industrial United States.

From the beginning, then, schooling was concerned with depriving youth of idle, free time and curing them of their vagrant and criminal inclinations. Compulsory attendance was not merely the forced attendance in state schools to learn the rudiment of reading, writing, and arithmetic. It was a program for training the youth of society in the behavioral norms of the workplace and factory. Schools had similar relationships and authority structures — the youngsters were taught to obey no matter what they were told to do. They were ordered to strive and compete even when their opportunities for success were severely limited by language and cultural differences. Different types of schools were established to provide tracks for youngsters from different social stations, thus, constraining and restricting their occupational opportunities. Still, the value of education as a pathway to economic opportunity persisted:

Is anyone willing to give an ignorant farm laborer as much as he is ready to pay for the services of an intelligent man? And if not, why the distinction? And if an ignorant man is not the best man upon a farm, is he likely to be so in a shop or mill? And if not, we see how the proprietors of factories are interested in elevating the standard of learning, in the mills and outside. But they are not singular in this. All classes of employers are equally concerned in the education of the laborer, for learning not only makes his labor more valuable to himself, but the market price of the product is generally reduced, and the change effects favorably all interests of society. This benefit is one of the first in point of time and the one, perhaps, most appreciable of all which learning has conferred upon the laborer. As each laborer, with the same expenditure of physical force, produces a greater result, of course the aggregate products of the world are vastly increased, although they represent only the same number of laborers that a less quantity would have represented under an ignorant system.[6]

Let us return for a moment to the first compulsory attendance proposals and to that edict of 1852 that led to compulsory attendance laws in most states of the Union by the end of the century. From the beginning, the laws set themselves the task of ameliorating the social disorganization that accompanied urban growth and massive immigration. Although these laws were largely unenforced during most of this time, they were used to reduce urban delinquency in some northeastern states. In 1846, the Massachusetts Senate committee on Establishing a Reform School declared:

If a child is brought up with thieves and drunkards, it will be singular, indeed, if he become not a thief or a drunkard or both; he may be educated to evil as well as good. If a child is friendless, homeless — or if his parents are vicious — he is easily led into temptation and induced, perhaps by want, perhaps by evil example, to commit some small theft. For this first crime, he will be carried before a court and sentenced to the House of Correction. If at this point he could be rescued, placed under the care of judicious men, taught to labor, be furnished with a good moral and intellectual training, he would, in nine cases out of ten, become a good and useful citizen. But we have no provision for such training. Instead of being disposed of, he is sent for a short time to associate with desperate and hardened criminals and is then returned upon the community with feelings hardened, his moral sense blunted, and the spirit of revenge burning in his bosom, it may be, against those whom he considers the instrument of his degradation. He has learnt caution, too: he will not be less likely to steal, but he will be more wary, until again grown bold by success he will perform some feat which will bring him once more before the court, to procure another sentence to the House of Correction, where he will take still another and deeper lesson in crime. What can be the result of such an education? . . . Clearly, a total depravity in morals and a life of wrong-doing, terminated in the State Prison or on the gallows.[7]

Crime and increasing pockets of urban poverty continued to worsen; during this period, the number of poor and immigrant families multiplied rapidly. However, it was not until 1849 that an alarming increase in the rate of crime caused the Boston School Committee to propose compulsory education for all children; it was decided that those Irish children who did not work in factories or attend schools were outside the reach and control of society.[8] A law subjecting them to arrest and incarceration in reform schools was strongly urged. Youngsters would be sent to such places for larceny, vagrancy, stubbornness, truancy, and so on. Soon, however, the number of truants in these children's prisons became overwhelming, with Irish immigrant boys being disproportionately represented; the Boston marshal began to compile statistics on the number of truant and vagrant boys in such reform schools, and it was shown that most were of foreign parentage.[9]

When the effects of industrialism became more oppressive prior to the outbreak of the Civil War, the problems of extreme poverty and idle, delinquent youth became more immediate. Still, it was not until the end of the century that compulsory education laws were effectively enforced.

This was the period of Horace Mann's writings on the value of educated labor in 1842 and of George S. Boutwell's papers on educated labor and industrialism in 1859. During this time, the world of labor was revolutionized yet again by the appearance of more sophisticated forms of machine technology and communications. As the size of business organizations grew, the need for literate, educated labor also increased. Yet, it was the increasing population of immigrant and urban poor families that prompted the Board of Public Charities of the State of Pennsylvania to propose compulsory education laws in 1871: a state with so many neglected children, a youth population rendered unemployable by ignorance and idle habits, was a danger to the social tranquility and peace of society. Their report proclaimed the duty of the state to look after and educate those unfortunate children who had nowhere else to turn.[10]

In this continuing struggle to gather in and educate the youth of the nation, the creation of compulsory education laws was certainly, as time went by, a victory for those who wanted to establish the common schools. For the first time, voluntary attendance was supplanted by legal coercion and the threat of confinement in reform schools or houses of correction. The culturally and intellectually deprived were not to be excluded from attendance in the common schools. Those youngsters who had little aptitude or taste for book learning were no longer excused. They were accepted into the classroom in the belief that every child could benefit from ordinary classroom discipline. A mutual system of responsibility was established between the states of the Union and the children who resided within those states. Youth had a right and an obligation to attend schools. States had a duty to provide such schooling for their young people.

URBAN CRIME AND DELINQUENCY

The first house for the reform of indigent and idle boys was opened in Boston in 1814. This Boston Asylum for Indigent Boys was not a true reform school in the modern sense: its inmates were not convicted of crimes by local magistrates; they were orphans and neglected children who private philanthropies wished to provide with a "judicious system of education."[11] Unfortunately, what had been a pressing concern about pauperism in the 1830s and 1840s became an ever-increasing social cancer from the late 1840s until the Depression of 1857. Every rural school and state reformatory constructed during this period was committed to an apprentice form of labor for its students and inmates. When the Massachusetts state legislature reported favorably on a petition to establish a state manual labor school in 1846, the school was benefitted by a $10,000 gift from Theodore Lyman, a former mayor of Boston. At Westborough, a school for 300 boys was constructed in 1848, and student-inmates were taught to do farm work and to make shoes and chairs. These reforms in the schooling and punishment of juveniles were an attempt to provide more humane treatment for offenders during a time when crime and poverty were exploding. It was thought that these social ills were an outgrowth of urbanism, with its many temptations and its lack of moral and community restraints on youngsters. In 1864, trustees of the reform school at Westborough reported that unless the ever-increasing numbers of delinquent boys were placed in "some such facility as this," they would "inevitably become a very dangerous class."[12] School reformers took notice of the fact that the first crimes of urban youth followed a pattern that led to more serious offenses against society as they grew older. First came truancy, then attendance in saloons, theatrical districts, and other places where "profanity, drunkenness and licentiousness" hurried youth down the path of "crime and ruin." "It is in the cities and large towns that the greater number of our state paupers are found," the legislative committee of the Massachusetts House noted in 1858. Faced with the unrelenting rise of urbanism and industrialism in towns and cities, the state authorities established almshouses. The inmates were from urban centers like Boston and Lowell. Of 7,100 inmates in state almshouses in 1858, 2,719 of them were from industrial centers.[13] As for the new urban areas themselves, as the legislative committee on charitable institutions observed, there were few of them that were not swarming with masses of paupers and poverty-stricken immigrants. The committee report asserted further:

Monster corporations import by the shipload the employees who fill their mills, do the base drudgery of their workshops and their degrading, ill-paid, menial services in every branch of business. They allow them to erect in their cities and towns the most miserable shanties for dwellings, or else the capitalists, who profit by their labor, do it in their stead. In them are made the paupers of the state.[14]

The purpose of the reform school was to provide a relief from these conditions of poverty, crime and family disorganization and dissolution. Children were capable of good or evil, as S. B. Woodward of the State Lunatic Hospital in Worcester wrote; it was

Absolutely important that the young be subjected to favorable impressions, and be trained in the course of virtue and duty, or the tendency will be unfavorable, and great hazard run, of a career of vice with individuals whose moral and intellectual culture has been neglected in childhood and early youth.[15]

THE REFORM SCHOOL

When the Westborough state reform school was opened in 1848, it was intended as a place that took "neglected, wayward children." It was "not to be called a prison or penitentiary." It was to be made to look as little as possible like a prison while insuring that student-inmates would not be able to escape their incarceration. The commissioners made a distinction between character formation and reform and punishment: "The fact must never be lost sight of that the prime object of the school is the reformation of the boy, and not his punishment. . . . It is to prevent him from becoming a criminal, and to make him a man."[16]

The same principles and aims of public education were affirmed by these school reformatories: "respect for authority, self-control, self-discipline, self-reliance, and self-respect."[17] The goal was, according to the Westborough's superintendent, the acquisition by the boy of a "fixed character" and a complete transfer of his inner personality and conscience.

Attempts were made to simulate family life in order to make the experience at Westborough more humane. According to Superintendent Joseph A. Allen in 1861, "The great design of the school should be to make it, as much as possible, like a family — to have the boys stand to the officers in the relation of children to parents."[18] Each cottage in the family system was supervised by a married couple who had the authority to manage and control the boys in their separate households. Sixty boys were given the opportunity to live in these domestic, homelike settings. Such efforts only affected the most compliant and cooperative of student-inmates, of course. Efforts were made to place boys on farms, where they could learn to perform productive labor. An attempt was made to counteract the vicious consequences of urban life, to provide student-inmates with the moral machinery they would need to succeed in their adult lives. Still, most student-inmates lived in more impersonal, prisonlike settings where tight scheduling, punitive discipline, and work filled most of their time. Why was this so? Was it a matter of cost consciousness and correct training or simply a way of keeping the more disturbing student-inmates occupied during their terms of imprisonment? If the latter, how to explain the apprentice system of labor that was emphasized by school officers? During the 1860s, the student-inmates made shoes and chairs. Of them, 20 percent worked on the school farm, 30 percent worked on sewing and knitting chores, 22 percent in chair work, and the rest in domestic types of labor. The chair making was for a private contractor, who paid "the school one and one-quarter cents per hour for the labor of each boy."[19] "What was the cause of crime and social disorder?" the school reformers of the time asked again and again, and they answered by citing the facts: it was urban life and the idleness, poverty, and vice created there.

The reform school at Westborough used confinement in a precise manner, making it an instrument of character reformation. Its goal was to teach boys to subordinate themselves and their desires to their responsibilities and duties in the reform school community. They wished to control the environment within which the student-inmates worked and studied and to act as a substitute parent. Education was thought to be in an invidious opposition to ignorance. One possessed a moral authority;

the other was almost akin to sinfulness itself. Education's effectiveness was affirmed in the offices and workshops of the nation. Ignorance's wages were paid in the penal colonies and prisons that sprang up everywhere. Since the beginning of recorded history, education had been the mark of breeding, culture, and class distinctions. It was not only these religious, social, and political needs that directed youth to learn in state schools, however. There were also the insistent needs of machine society and its aftermath: technological changes in production and communications foster new bureaucratic organizations and a need for educated employees.

The obligation to reform the delinquent and incorrigible youth of Massachusetts was used by reformers as a justification for establishing Westborough and the common schools. The Board of State Charities believed that social reform had to come through an "enlightenment of conscience" of the prosperous as well as the indigent citizens of the commonwealth. Here is their admonition, concluding their 1865 report:

People had to understand the basic causes of poverty and crime so they could "take interest and direct action in social improvement, by leveling from below upward." Where "the degree of poverty which excludes education exists, it abases and finally destroys self-respect, which breeds diseases, indolence and vice. The property of all becomes unsafe and the morals of the community weakened."[20] Reformers believed that authority, kindliness, enlightenment of conscience, and constant labor were the four primary elements in the reformation process. This commitment to purposeful activity, to which religion and industrial society were both deeply bound, had as its counterpoint a hatred of aimlessness and idleness. Those who waited for charity, luck, or God to come to their aid in this life were sinful, because they disobeyed the commandment of the Scriptures: "Thou shalt not tempt the Lord thy God." As Calvin had taught, the reluctance of the poor and delinquent youth to work meant that they were "trying beyond measure the power of God." They were seeking a miracle, but the miracle of labor and labor's rewards were granted to man every day of his life. If it is true that idleness is the pathway to evil and sin, then purposeful work is the way to a realization of God's will on earth. This was why idleness was considered akin to rebellion by the good people of Boston: it burdened them with a sinful and ever-increasing welfare population. Idleness was the sin of man in the Garden of Eden, but the sin was more acutely felt in a newly industrialized United States. In the factories, where the workers had to be as disciplined as their machines, idleness and insubordination were disastrous defects. We must not forget that the law establishing the Westborough reform school spoke out against mendicancy and idleness of urban delinquents. Idleness and the poor were closely associated in the minds of the wealthier citizens of the nation.

It was not surprising, then, that urban delinquents were incarcerated in reform schools that emphasized discipline, work, and obedience. From its origins, student-inmates were forced to follow strict routines, schedules, and work assignments or be punished by more severe forms of confinement and harassment. A group of boys were found manacled in dismal "unsanitary cells" by one investigating team, and in 1860, one newspaper described the "method of treatment . . . the vulgar and harsh method of convict discipline, enforced by the carrying of bludgeons and loaded weapons by some of the officers" that existed in the institution.[21] Like adult prisoners, student-inmates were forced to accept the conditions of forced labor.

In the workshops where they toiled, boys were graded for reliability and productivity, and those who could be trusted were sometimes sent to the farm school. The other 90 percent and more of the student-inmates were confined in cells and provided with a regime designed especially for urban delinquents. By the mid 1850s, education was firmly linked to social purposefulness and progress in the minds of many Americans. Schools of all kinds condemned youth who were disruptive and unresponsive to organizational schedules and routines, suspending and transferring the worst offenders.

It is important to say that the relationship between the practice of compulsory attendance and routines and the insistence that the work be done in regimented ways was defined in large measure by the need for social order and control in overcrowded urban schools. It also fit the needs of a mechanistic world of work for disciplined, robotic workers. A moral perception supported and sustained the practices of public schools, as we have seen. When the leaders of school reform published their reports on the poor, it was made quite clear that the condition of their poverty was a consequence of their weak self-discipline and moral laxness. Both the common schools and the first reform school at Westborough were a way of rendering immigrant and urban youth more obedient and useful in an industrial society.

It is in this context that the growing urban poor were viewed as more of a moral dilemma than an economic one by the early reformers. Therefore, the school was not merely a place where the delinquent and poor were kept out of the labor market and off the city's streets. The student-inmate who could and would accept the authority and routines of the reform school would be released after a year or two, not so much because he would be less impoverished in the outside world but because he had accepted the ethical standards and economic structures of the adult world. Schools specified that work must occupy the greater part of the day and must be interspersed with readings from pious books. It was this moral basis that gave schoolmasters and reform school officers their legitimacy and also gave them the right to observe, judge, and punish infractions in the name of society and the youth's own welfare. It was only when student-inmates or students accepted the unquestioned pedagogic authority of the adult staff that they could be taught the things they needed to know. Finally, every fault was to be punished by a reduction of rations, by an increase in laboring time, by incarceration in state manual schools, and by other punishments that fit different infractions.

THE REFORM SCHOOL AT WESTBOROUGH

Let us look again at the first reform school at Westborough and the reputation this school had prior to the Civil War. It was described as an austere and forbidding institution, a disciplinary children's prison that functioned every waking moment of a student-inmate's day: all phases of a boy's life were programmed by officers at the school. Special attention was given to the student-inmate's values, his everyday deportment, his ability to master the work and curriculum, and his state of mind. The reform school was an ever-present presence, observing, judging, and punishing. Moreover, its isolated physical location meant that once boys were confined there, their training could not be interrupted until they were finally released. The discipline was unending. Officers had complete control over the bodily movements and lives of youngsters. Their methods of regimentation and repression were part of a penal and oppressive regime. In this sense, the reform school was the common school carried to impossible extremes. Its practices were deemed necessary if urban and immigrant youth were to be purged of their perverted and delinquent ways. The constraint of an educational apparatus that functioned unceasingly was needed to counteract the previous life experiences of the student-inmate. The freedom and time of the boy was tightly controlled by school officers. For days, months, and years, the time of the student-inmate was scheduled, waking and going to bed, activity and rest, time set aside for meals, the kind and quality of food, the work and manual labor, prayer, the right to speak and to think, walks from one location in the building to the next. Such education took complete control of the student-inmate's mind and body, achieving the total institutional effect.[22]

The primary mechanism of control at Westborough was isolation from the everyday world of the outside community, from those influences that had motivated the delinquency, truancy, or depravity of the student-inmate. The youngsters were kept apart from one another, too. Plots and revolts and immoral associations were forbidden inside the reform school. Isolated in his dismal cell, the boy was expected to reflect upon his criminal behavior. His confinement forced him to face the transgression he had committed against society, to feel remorse. The punishment was experienced as a personal trauma: the separation from society and his fellow student-inmates was seen as the cruelest of penalties.

The reform school provided boys with cells where they could sleep at night and rooms where they could do work and eat meals. Silence was the rule that could not be broken, the boys being permitted to speak only when officers allowed them to do so. This reflected the demands of the workplace as well as those of order and control in the children's prison. The reform school was to be a small school in which boys were transformed into moral individuals. Relations with other student-inmates were discouraged. Constraint was administered by constant surveillance and punishment; boys were forced to mingle in education and work activities but not to talk to one another. Their behavior was pressed into a mold of useful, purposeful labor and silence. Their actions were constantly monitored and supervised in order to reform them as social persons. Their training aimed at changing them into law-abiding, productive workers and citizens.

Nevertheless, the ideas of conscience and moral thinking were prominent in the thought of those who sought to rehabilitate these urban delinquents. Solitude would be used as the punishment of last resort, the place where a boy would be forced to face himself and his aberrant behavior. The punishment of the law was but one part of the process; the inner self of the boy must be reformed as well. He must submit to his conscience as well as to the training of the reformatory. A moral awakening was demanded. The children's prison was the place of punishment, the cell the place where the student-inmate reflected upon his past and where he came face-to-face with his conscience. Schoolwork was more than just the learning of manual skills and knowledge. It was the means by which correct moral thinking was encouraged. Officers did not have to use physical force alone. Their power and authority, like that of the schoolteacher in common schools, was justified and supported by a moral ethos that was shared by most Americans.

Transformation, then, was the goal of the reform school, isolation and confinement the method. Mass reformatories were more economical, more desirable, and more humane. This meant that officers had to be overly concerned with surveillance and control. An attempt was made to prohibit and eliminate any relationship between boys that was not originated or supervised by those in authority inside the reform school.

There was a continuous schedule of manual labor and schoolwork, meals, and religious instruction, and then eight hours of regulated sleep in the evenings. Days were devoted to instruction and work. Time was, thus, made to stand still as the days, weeks, and years followed with an institutional sameness. The truant and urban delinquent was now forced into a regular routine, a habit of acknowledging time and organized controls that were designed to wean him away from his vices and criminal inclinations. Schooling was an integral part of this reformation of the spirit, as we have shown. It made the boy more employable and, so, less likely to commit crimes against the social order. Work was at the center of the reform school, the method by which the student-inmate was confined and corrected while participating in a form of penal labor.

Nominal wages were paid to the reform school for the work that was done by the boys. Their labor was simply not rewarded. In this way, the work became part of the punishment, because boys were not allowed to refuse to do it.

Work had the effect of ordering the urban delinquent's life and providing him with regularity. Its demands were received as those emanating from a powerful, unseen social force. Again, the mind and body of the student-inmate were coerced into responding to schedules and timetables in the institution. Aimless behavior and distractions were not tolerated, and a hierarchy observed every movement. With work, the rules and regulations took on a sacrosanct aura, supported as they were by repression and physical coercion and punishment. By demanding that work be attended to, the boy was trained to obey, the idler was taught to be active, and the demands of the schedule were observed. Forced labor was a vital part of the reform school's transformation process. It helped to change antisocial, violent, and criminal youth into obedient, compliant workers and citizens. The work in school filled a great deal of the time for boys, tending to mechanize them according to the needs of labor in machine society. Also, it was paid for in moral wages that permitted the youngster to survive inside the institution.

The organizational structures and practices of this reform school were almost certainly influenced by the charity schools and reform schools of an earlier period. The silent productivity also had its beginnings in the religious communities of the distant past. Still, the reform school did more than merely incarcerate the immigrant and urban delinquents. It individualized penalties by supervising and transforming the student-inmate's character, by rejecting him as he was in favor of some normal and accepted form of social behavior.

Delinquents and truants were punished similarly. The gravity of their offenses was mentioned only in the courts and papers that committed them to the state reform school. There was one standard for all, one vision once they were confined in the children's prison.

Of course, there were the dangerous and violent realities of such a prison school. Four phases of adjustment can be mentioned here. There was a time of initial intimidation. This was followed by a period of adjustment to the work and living routines. Then came a phase of moral indoctrination and a period of institutional adjustment to the preferred behavior patterns of the school The routines of the reformatory were accomplished by a system of rewards and punishments and by officers who carried loaded firearms at their sides.

There was a disconnection, then, between those who sent boys to the reform school and those who actually enforced their detention once they were in these children's prisons. The officers had complete control over what happened to boys and how they were punished when infractions were committed. They had the day-to-day responsibility to carry through the legal mandate of the courts. They were the ones who judged student-inmate's deportment — they watched, they assessed, they characterized, they informed, and they classified. They were the ones who judged when reformation had been accomplished and when a boy ought to be considered for the farm school or released.

The construction of this children's prison was an important innovation in schooling's practices. It was a place where administrative force was used to constrain and confine adolescents for moral, social, and economic considerations. For the first time, a compulsory school emphasizing education, vocational training, and moral and ethical transformation was established. Duty to society and penal servitude were united in one experience. The children's prison meant that pauper boys and neglected children would no longer be allowed to wander about the streets of industrial cities and towns. Of course, this was not the first time that criminal behavior, even in its most questionable form of truancy, idleness, and stubbornness, had been made into a transgression against the laws of the state, but in this incarceration of urban delinquents, the important point — and the uniqueness of the occurrence — was that boys were confined in reformatories, where the law was used with resolute purpose, without concession, and in the most severe forms of mental and physical restraint. Moral virtue was to be taught to these urban juvenile offenders at any cost.

Thus, we see inscribed in the reform school the belief that good behavior is a concern of government and adult society. The buildings of the children's prison were built in the conviction that correct behavior and a respect for authority and property could be taught to boys in schools, either common ones or reformatories. The isolated structures were the opposite of society's dream of individual liberty and freedom for all. At the center of the school reform school credo was this idea that correct behavior in boys was mandated by force without appeal, that the officers were agents of societal values and beliefs, and that their intimidating actions were performed in the name of the state of Massachusetts and for the greater good of the boys themselves. This is the darker side of the school reformer's appeals for compulsory education attendance laws. The laws of states were an attempt to deal with profound social and economic problems by applying an educational adjustment to the children of the common people and the poor.

Was this not the same dilemma that haunted the founders of the first charity schools in New York and Philadelphia? One of the requirements at Westborough was to see to it that religious instruction was properly pursued. The officers must teach the student-inmates about religious practice and see to it that they read from the Scriptures. They must, of course, teach them also the rudiments of language, arithmetic, and a trade with which they could make their way in the world of work once they were released from the reformatory. They must make sure that the boys attended and showed proper reverence at weekly religious services in the chapel.

The reform school was a social and legal response to the pressing problems that accompanied industrialization in the middle and late nineteenth century. From the beginning, it had the reputation that seemed to separate it from the common schools of the nation. As a penal response to urban delinquency and as a social reaction to the mounting poverty and crime in cities, it had questionable success, but in the history of public schooling, it signaled an important turning point: the moment in time when education was used by the state as an important instrument in the struggle against widening urban poverty, idleness, and vice. This was the moment when education began to separate and control urban delinquents in age-graded, prison schools. The meanings reformers gave to poverty, the importance they attached to education as a need for all children, and all the ethical values attached to the preparation and performance of productive labor defined the kind of educational experiences children would have in common schools and reformatories. Education was, thus, made to serve the needs and interests of an increasingly rationalized and mechanistic society. Not so many years earlier, that society had basked in an agrarian culture and philosophy with an endless frontier before it. In Thomas Jefferson, in Lewis and Clark, in the endless possibilities of life in the New World could be found the basis for the emerging U.S. culture, but in less than a generation, schooling and work had been mechanized, and in the urban centers, immigrant and poor workers huddled together in increasing misery and despair.

NOTES

1. Michael B. Katz, *A History of Compulsory Education Laws* (Bloomington, Ind.: Phi Delta Kappa Educational Foundation, 1976), pp. 17–18; David Tyack, *The One Best System: A History of American Urban Education* (Cambridge, Mass.: Harvard University Press, 1974), p. 9.

2. Ellwood P. Cubberley, *The History of Education* (Cambridge, Mass.: Houghton-Mifflin, 1920), pp. 21–24.

3. David B. Tyack, *Turning Points in American History* (Waltham, Mass.: Blaisdell Publishing, 1967), pp. 14–17).

4. Cubberley, *The History of Education*, pp. 29–31.

5. David Nasaw, *Schooled to Order* (New York: Oxford University Press, 1979), pp. 81–82; Samuel Bowles and Herbert Gintis, *Schooling in Capitalist America* (New York: Basic Books, 1976), pp. 152–56.

6. Michael B. Katz, *School Reform: Past and Present* (Boston, Mass.: Little, Brown, 1971), pp. 151–52.

7. Ibid., pp. 43–44; Lawrence A. Cremin, *Traditions of American Education* (New York: Basic Books, 1977), pp. 126–28.

8. Katz, *School Reform: Past and Present*, pp. 47–48; Steven Lukes, *Emile Durkheim: His Life and Work* (New York: Harper and Row, 1972), pp. 109–12.

9. David Rothman, *The Discovery of the Asylum* (Boston, Mass.: Little, Brown, 1971), p. 262.

10. Stanley K. Schultz, *The Culture Factory* (New York: Oxford University Press, 1973), pp. 298–300.

11. David Owen, *English Philanthrophy 1660–1960* (Cambridge, Mass.: Little, Brown, 1964), pp. 152–55.

12. Michael B. Katz, *The Irony of School Reform* (Cambridge, Mass.: Harvard University Press, 1968), pp. 185–94.

13. Katz, *The Irony of School Reform*, pp. 172–74; David Tyack, "Ways of Seeing: An Essay on the History of Compulsory Schooling," *Harvard Educational*

Review 46 (August 1976): 367–68.

14. Katz, *The Irony of School Reform* p. 173; Merle Curti, *The Social Ideas of American Educators* (Totowa, N.J.: Littlefield Adams, 1963), pp. 119–21.

15. Katz, *The Irony of School Reform* pp. 43–44; see Diane Ravitch, *The Great School Wars: New York City 1805–1973* (New York: Basic Books, 1974) for an alternative picture of these events.

16. David W. Lewis, *From Newgate to Dannemora: The Rise of the Penitentiary in New York 1796–1848* (Ithaca, N.Y.: Cornell University Press, 1965), p. 201.

17. Joseph A. Allen, *Westborough State Reform School Reminiscences* (Boston, Mass.: Little, Brown, 1877), pp. 12–15.

18. Katz, *The Irony of School Reform*, pp. 188–89.

19. Ibid., pp. 194–95.

20. Allen, *Westborough State Reform School Reminiscences*.

21. Katz, *The Irony of School Reform*, pp. 195–96.

22. Ibid., p. 199.

3

Schooling the Poor

In its diverse manifestations, immigration to the United States fell into two distinct periods. At first the settlers were English, with the exception of a small Dutch settlement at New Amsterdam and a colony of Swedish Lutherans in the area now known as the state of Delaware. The dominance of pure English names is shown most clearly in the census of 1790, in which 83 percent of the population were so recorded. Only a handful of non-English-speaking colonists were in existence at this time.[1]

In fact, immigration before 1820 was insignificant and consisted mostly of white, Anglo-Saxon Protestants. The distinguishing characteristic of the new arrivals before 1840 was most often their indigent condition. In 1842, 100,000 migrants entered the United States. Thereafter, immigration never fell below 100,00 in any one year for the rest of the century. In the decade from 1847 to 1857, the number of newcomers was never less than 200,000, and in 1854, it reached 420,833 persons. From 1820 to 1840, immigration of German and Irish people took place, creating a crisis over Catholic parochial schools in Massachusetts. This was the beginning of the second phase of the immigration story, because the Irish were considered to be of different and inferior racial stock. The Germans, on the other hand, proved to be more acceptable. They were thought to be not much different in origin from the first English colonists themselves: courageous, intelligent, resourceful, adaptable, and self-reliant persons. The situation reached a critical point after 1882, when the character and background of the immigrants changed significantly. Armies of silent poor migrated from southern and eastern Europe. By 1890, 20,000 Italians were arriving every year, and from 1906 to 1910, as many as 1,180,000 reached U.S. shores. In the decade between 1903 and 1914, immigration reached 750,000 to 1,250,000 newcomers. After 1880, a host of nationalities from Austria, Poland, and the Balkans, Jews from Russia, and Japanese and Koreans from Asia swelled the tide of immigration. Many more people came from all parts of Europe and Canada.

The southern and eastern Europeans, however, were thought to be racially different and innately inferior to native U.S. stock. They were seen as illiterate, passive people with little self-initiative. They had no conception of Anglo-Saxon culture, with its ideas of liberty, law, government, and public decency. They weakened and corrupted the political processes of the Republic. These foreigners settled in the Northern cities and in the Midwest and Far West, creating a serious problem in housing, sanitary conditions, and the like because of their slovenly life styles. Public education found it difficult to accommodate these newcomers because, most often, they did not even speak the English language. Foreign mannerisms, customs, and language became dominant in some urban communities, and the schools were given the formidable task of transforming and Americanizing this foreign rabble.[2] By 1910, the census showed 10,000,000 and more foreign-born persons living in the United States. Many could not read or write, and their patriotism was openly questioned by indigenous Americans. The newcomers tended to huddle together in ghettos, where they could speak their native languages; even their children were sometimes sent to non-English-speaking parochial schools.

ASSIMILATION AS AN EDUCATIONAL GOAL

The schools were given the job of assimilating these alien peoples into the mainstream of U.S. life. They were to provide them with a command of English, an understanding of common law, government, freedom, and free schools, and a tolerance for others. These goals were in addition to their already-stated ones of socializing and transforming urban youth into compliant and productive workers and citizens. Now it was also their function to mitigate the separating tendencies of alien languages and cultures by providing immigrant and urban poor children with a common training that Americanized them and gave them access to better employment in the labor market.

Immigrant children were crowded into classrooms of immense size, often with children much younger than they.[3] They were often forced to sit in seats that were intended for eight-year-olds until they could learn to read and work in English; they then were sent to other crowded classrooms that were on their grade level, classrooms that often had 60 and more students in them.

Those students who were forced to sit in silence and obey without question were described as "wretched refuse" by the inscription that welcomed them on the Statue of Liberty. Education, at this point in its history, was asked to make loyal "Americans, productive workers, and affluent citizens out of . . . human garbage."[4] This view of the immigrant children as alien, inferior, and incompetent persons predominated in public schools and gave these institutions their somber ambience, their look of penal servitude.

Education was less than ever linked to learning alone. At its center were the correction and reformation of the immigrant child's language, culture, moral outlook, and inner self. The foreignness of immigrant youth could be altered only by severe discipline and a rejection of his parental heritage and values. The theme of the Americanized immigrant was effectively projected during this period in an attempt to gain support from the newcomers themselves. Education was held in high esteem by many of the families, and adults often attended night school in an effort to master the English language and earn their citizenship.

A moment had come in the history of U.S. education when, from this view of urban and immigrant youth as aliens and potential sources of social disorder and delinquency, a punitive discipline and pedagogy was formalized and practiced in urban schools throughout the nation. Still, education had an ever-increasing value for the immigrants. That value was closely linked to their desire to become full-fledged Americans and to learn the ways of their new country. However, those hopes were never fully realized. Education did not prove to be a panacea for the social and economic dislocations of industrial society. The discipline of schooling produced only barely literate citizens. It made the immigrant students more fully aware of just how unacceptable they and their families were to native-born Americans and how far they had to go before they would be considered real Americans. For the newcomers, the value of education lay in the teaching of English and the opportunities such learnings had for them in the labor markets of the industrialized United States. For them, the socialization in schools was an obvious rejection of their past heritages, which they often shared with school authorities. What was more painful, however, was the gulf that schooling often established between the young and their immigrant mothers and fathers. The ultimate goal was Americanization and the supplanting of English for native European languages and culture. All efforts were focused on these goals of student transformation, and the history, worthiness, and personal identities of immigrants and their children were ignored.

All these linguistic and cultural rejections of youngsters and their families, these practices woven into the very fabric of urban schooling, these usages that sanctified silence, uniformity, and obedience reduced youth to a mechanical, rote-learning educational experience. In public schools, education embraced the organizational structures and forms of punitive institutions of correction. It was separated from the community, and its work was accomplished in enclosed classrooms. Learning was treated as an esoteric domain of experts and professionals who had been certified by the state. It acted as the legitimate agent of the industrial United States, providing a harsh and uniformed learning experience for all. It was the exclusive and natural agency for the acculturation and transformation of youth, and it was so accepted by school authorities and the public alike.

STUDENT SUBORDINACY

Let us examine the role of the student as it was seen by schoolteachers during the latter half of the nineteenth century. The student was someone who could be easily identified by his age and demeanor inside the school building. He was a child or youth. The sign of his immaturity and dependency, the air of his subordinacy was apparent to even the most casual of observers. His body was stiff and alert to the demands of schoolteachers. He had to learn his role again and again in different classrooms with different teachers: when he could move or talk, where he could sit or stand, how he should perform his assigned tasks, what he should consider important, and so on. Most students appeared to their teachers as disinterested inattentive innocents who tended toward idleness and aimless play if left to their own devices. "Habits of obedience, attention, promptness in recitation, neatness of copybooks, and a carefully planned program of daily work" were some of the "characteristics and attractions of most schools," wrote Samuel King, the first superintendent of the Portland, Oregon, schools in 1875.[5] Children should display "a military air and discipline" in their movements and schoolwork. Thomas L. Eliot, a school superintendent of Multnomah County schools, wrote in 1873:

"Economy and efficiency in our schools depends in great degree upon a proper division of responsibilities. As in the army, so here."[6] Students must be forced to drill and work in unison with one another, because as men, they would have to work together in large workshops, factories, offices, or military organizations.

By the late 1880s, the common man with an elementary education of some sort was being produced throughout the nation. Youngsters were viewed by adults and educators alike as formless, semiaware persons who could be molded for good or evil, for idleness or productivity. The educated, literate adult could be manufactured. New students became accustomed to maintaining a military posture in their classrooms, to looking adults in the eye when they were spoken to, to standing at attention without lowering their head, to providing bodily and verbal assurances to teachers that they were not defiant or menacing in any way.

The schools focused their energies on controlling the bodily movements of the learner, thus, gaining complete power over him. It is easy enough to discover the many rules and regulations that manipulated, corrected, and trained students to respond and to obey. The control of the individual youngster was accomplished on two levels: the ethical belief systems of the culture held in common by teachers, parents, and students provided a moral basis for the students' compliance with authority's demands, and the organizational schedules, timetables, and guidelines controlled, corrected, and directed their every movement and thought inside the building. These two modes of domination were complimentary because they were the moral and ethical force justifying student subordinacy in the school. In Ellwood P. Cubberley's opinion, the schools in 1908 were

Factories in which the raw materials (children) are to be shaped and fashioned into products to meet the various demands of life. The specifications for manufacturing come from the demands of the 20th century civilization, and it is the business of the school to build its pupils to the specifications laid down.[7]

And, of course, there were many instances in which the two systems of culture and organization came together, as in the goal of creating submissive, obedient, and useful workers and citizens. A student's body was deemed to be properly compliant when it could be ordered about, directed, and transformed into an organizationally acceptable and useful being.

This concern with the bodily movements of students was not something new in educational practice, of course. In public schools and other organizations in society, the mind and body of the member or worker were strictly controlled by powerful social, economic, and religious forces. However, the schools introduced an old idea into the equation of compulsory education: to treat the student's body as though it was a mechanical unit that required assigned places and uniform, regimenting forms of movement and work inside the school building. Joseph Rice wrote in 1892 of the extreme military routines that characterized urban public schools in the East and Midwest. President Charles W. Eliot of Harvard attacked mass education, which "almost inevitably adopts military or mechanistic methods," that same year.[8]

Students were controlled by distinct levels of organizational discipline. Their movements, gestures and work were closely scheduled, supervised, and evaluated according to prevailing standards. The focus of control was no longer only the language and cultural understandings of the child. The student's economy and efficiency in completing his assigned tasks or moving from one classroom to another were also regulated and assessed. There were also the inevitable modalities of discipline that were common in overcrowded, industrial institutions and society. They dictated a constant use of authority, observing and judging each action of the student rather than merely his final educational achievements.

A code was developed in these schools that partitioned the time frames, spatial locations, and movements of students inside the school building. These schedules and regulations made it possible for teachers to control the behaviors and movements of a student's body, thus, assuring its continuous submission to the discipline and authority imposed upon it.

The students' condition differed from that of indentured servants or slaves because their bodies were not appropriated on a full-time basis. They could be made to do things only if they were in the accepted realm of educational practice. Their teachers were mentors and models, not masters in the sense of having unlimited power over them. From the vassalage of the past, from the military, penal, and religious communities of history, from monasteries had come a science of mastery over the mind and body of the individual in modern society. This science was not concerned with the development of learning and educational knowledge alone or with student subjugation but with the formation of a mechanism that made youngsters more amenable and compliant to the demands of pedagogic authority. What was created in public schools was an organizational structure that coerced the body of the student and manipulated his movements, thought, gestures, and behavior in the interest of orderly movement and instruction. The student's social status in the larger community and in the school was clearly identified and labeled so that the schools could make rational decisions about his progress through the grades.

An agency of social and economic restraint and reproduction was established that also simulated the despotism of the workplace. It defined who had power over whom, at what places, and during what periods of time. This was to insure an efficiency in the performance of educational tasks. Horace Mann had made this point in 1842 in his "Fifth Report of the Secretary Board."[9] When the youngsters became men, they would work "side by side, in the same factory, at the same machinery, in making the same fabrics, and, by a fixed rule of the establishment, labor the same number of hours each day." The common schools were to be a training ground for the establishment of docile, useful workers who would not refuse to do the repetitive, meaningless work of the nation's factories and bureaucracies. The new discipline in schools was to produce well-trained workers and well-adjusted citizens. Such discipline made youngsters more purposeful and utilitarian while diminishing their will to resist the prevailing authority structures. The power to control one's body was now transformed into a student's aptitude or capability in the school building, which he was duty-bound to improve. His role and status were reduced to that of an unskilled laborer in a factory or worse. The child entered an organized ethos that standardized the work, rationalized it, and graded it. An ethos of control that was validated by the needs of the mass school and society itself was created. It defined how and why educators could have a hold over the bodily movements and attention of students. It determined how and why youngsters had to do what they were told with speed and dispatch. Thus, schools simulated the conditions of the workplace by producing compliant, responsive individuals. School discipline sought to increase the efficiency of students while making them more willing to do meaningless work without protesting or simply walking away from it.[10]

CLASSROOM DISCIPLINE AND PUNISHMENT

Discipline in public schools required enclosed classrooms where students were assigned a seat and closet space. The classroom was the place where school routines were drilled into the youngster's head along with an arbitrary school culture and pedagogy. There was the confinement of the children according to their age and grade. There were the special areas of assembly. There was the military model of uniform classrooms placed side by side along common corridors. And, of course, there was the parade of students from place to place. Urban and immigrant youth, that malleable mass, had to be kept under constant surveillance and control; fighting and disorder must be prevented; the language and customs of immigrants must be transformed; conflict with teachers must be punished. The establishment of overcrowded urban schools, often enclosed by metal fencing, became more common. These urban schools were openly compared with workshops and factories. Teachers were urged to treat students as if they were workers, and a bell was used to announce the beginning and end of work periods. Late-comers were disciplined and their offenses recorded; teachers were asked to identify truants for correctional officers. The goal was to encourage purposeful work and to eliminate aimlessness and work interruptions or disturbances of any kind. The children were taught to work in more concentrated ways, and to protect the materials and property of the school.

Still, enclosure alone was not enough to sustain the school's pedagogic and disciplinary system. Partitioning of area locations was necessary, also. Pluralities, groups, and collectivities were broken down into individual entities. The distribution of space had to be detailed and precise;[11] student appearances at different places in the school building had to be authorized by teachers or administrators. It was important to avoid cutting, truancy, and other acts of delinquency and defiance. The goal was to establish a propriety of presence so that teacher would be able to locate students during the school day, to place the conduct of each youngster under constant scrutiny, to be in a position to challenge and calculate its merits. Discipline was the practice of observing status positions inside the building, a technique for asserting, once again, the rights of adult rank and authority over children.

In his report on the nature and functioning of public schools during the last half of the nineteenth century, Charles Adams described the overcrowded classrooms of immigrants and native children in Quincy, Massachusetts:

Most of you, indeed, cannot but have been part and parcel of one of those huge, mechanical, educational machines, or mills, as they might more properly be called. They are, I believe, peculiar to our own time and country, and are so organized as to combine as nearly as possible the principal and characteristics of the cotton mill and the railroad with those of the model state prison. The school committee is the board of directors, while the superintendent — the chief executive officer— sits in his central office with the timetable, which he calls a programme, before him, by which one hour twice a week is allotted to this study, and half an hour three times a week to that, and twenty hours a term to a third; and at such a time one class will be at this point and the other class at that, the whole moving with military precision to a given destination at a specified date. . . . From one point of view children are regarded as automatoms; from another, as India-rubber bags; from a third, as so much raw material.[12]

In the schools that appeared at the end of the 1800s, when bureaucratic ideas were being codified, the idea of partitioning became more sophisticated. It was important to locate students so that they were distinct units that could be placed on a map of the school building. The distribution of students in such schools, the graded work schedules, and the standardized pedagogic work of teachers had to be coordinated by a central authority.

Public School 122 in Manhattan, New York, constructed after the Civil War, exemplified these principles of partition and enclosure.[13] It was four stories high and contained many rectangular, uniform classrooms. The ground floor was essentially a staging area; the second, third, and fourth floors housed classrooms with desks and chairs bolted firmly to the floor and arranged in six rows, with large windows set 4.5 feet above the floor. Each student worked at his or her desk with croquill pens that periodically needed refilling from desk inkwells. There were classes of 36 to 48 and more in these somber rooms. Around the classroom were bulletin boards and blackboards where the best student work was often displayed. By moving up and down the rows of seats, the teacher could observe and correct students who were malingering or otherwise not doing things in the prescribed manner. She could supervise the student's movements and purposefulness and the neatness and accuracy of his schoolwork. She could make judgments and comparisons with other students, seating them according to the speed, accuracy, and skill of their test scores and deportment. She kept records, of course, on the different levels of attainment that a youngster achieved during the school year. All of these gradations formed a schedule of student development and accomplishments. Each step was simplified and separated from another, dividing education into a series of uniform, graded tasks. Youngsters were then estimated according to their place on this achievement scale. Each factor was to be observed, assessed, and judged in comparison with other students — perseverance, ability,

promptness, diligence, and so on. Thus, the individuals in a classroom
or school could be analyzed and assessed as separate units. This
division of the educational process into small, rationalized tasks
mirrored the emergence of large-scale industry and bureaucracy in the
world of work.

In the discipline of the school or workplace, however, the key consideration was not the locations of individuals, their scheduling, or the
timetables that regulated their movements. The key was always the
social standing or rank of the individual as he or she interacted with
others in the school building, workshop, or factory. Discipline in these
repressive settings was always a mater of rank and station. It allowed for
the control of members no matter where they were encountered in the
institution.

The class was one important example of this control. One found an
educational unit that was divided into meticulous parts. The rows of
seats, which could accommodate eight students, were assigned
according to achievement and conduct, as we have already mentioned.
The form was that of a constant competition and weekly revision of the
seating order and rank arrangement. Schoolwork was performed as a
struggle to improve one's status and rank at the expense of fellow
students. The work of individual youngsters was recorded and maintained throughout the school year. It allowed the teacher to calculate
average scores for every student and to assign seating places and grades
that reflected overall standings in the class. Supervisors and visitors
could tell at a glance which children were doing well and which were
not. Subjects were taught in an order of increasing difficulty, so that the
ranks of pupils coincided with their age and seniority in the school. Of
course, the rank and status of adults were always higher than those of
any student.

SCHEDULES, TIMETABLES, AND
PREPARING FUTURE WORKERS

Let us look again at the schedules and timetables that controlled the
overcrowded urban schools of the nineteenth century.[14] These
mechanisms of social order and control were derived from coercive
communities of the past and the new needs of the industrial
United States. They found a natural acceptance in the overcrowded
schools. Their essential features were soon to be found in factories,
hospitals, asylums, workshops, and bureaucracies. They helped
authorities to establish rhythms, to impose graded, individual tasks and

responsibilities, and to routinize tasks through the use of pedagogies that emphasized rote learning and constant repetition. These public schools found it convenient to embrace these old instruments of domination because of their peculiar problems. They were indispensable in ordering and controlling the diverse immigrant and poor populations that now overwhelmed public education. In the last decades of the nineteenth century, the school day was planned with greater care than ever before. However, even then, schools were merely imitating the conditions of work in adult society. In the factories of Henry Ford that were built in the early years of the twentieth century, worker discipline was achieved through the assembly line that moved past workers with deliberate speed. Factory life had the effect of linking the worker to the time frame and rhythms of his machine. The schools found their own way of simulating these conditions by using schedules and timetables to regiment and order the temporal life of students in the institution. They partitioned the time into periods of work. This happened most in the new secondary schools, of course. There, the systematic scheduling of time into arrivals, departures, and periods of activities was most formal and severe. In the elementary schools, the timetable was more precise but less formal; activities were begun and ended at the teacher's command. At the sound of a bell, pupils would line up in the assembly area and, on command, walk in orderly lines to their homeroom classes with their heads facing directly in front of them and in silence. When the attendance had been taken and coats put away, the teacher signaled when students were to bow their head in prayer or stand to salute the flag. Also, an attempt was made to assure that the time spent during the school day was well used. Continual scrutiny, correction, and assessment by teachers tried to assure the quality of time spent in different activities and lessons. Distractions of any kind were discouraged. A collective and imposed rhythm was demanded by teachers. It was their method of getting children to perform their work together. It assured that they would do the same work at the same time, and it made it much easier for teachers to control the students.

We have now moved from the simple ordering and control of students to methods of standardizing and evaluating classwork in a competitive ethos. A social sorting machine allowed teachers to identify and reward successful students while punishing unsuccessful ones. The education of youth was broken down into a number of routinized, graded tasks that had to be accomplished according to the school's timetables. The level of development was defined and articulated by teachers at least three times each term. To each student's work the teacher assigned a valuation, a rank. Student success assured promotion to the next grade and more difficult schoolwork.

Hence, the need to control the gestures and responses of these immigrant and urban poor children. School discipline did not merely seek to teach or impose an arbitrary language and culture on students. It sought also to train their bodies in prompt and efficient reactions to the commands presented by the impositional teacher. In the proper use of the self, which makes possible the best use of time, no energies must be wasted on aimless or purposeless activities. Everything must be done to establish machinelike responses to the demands of higher authorities and schoolteachers.

In the elementary school, the lessons of the period began with a command from the teacher; until then, the students were engaging in waiting behavior. They could not begin their day until the important person in the learning situation called the class to order. When she called out "Class!," each student sat up a little straighter in his or her seat, "straight as a ramrod, eyes front, hands clasped rigidly" in military fashion.[15] At the core of the school's discipline was its regulation of student behavior not covered by the law or district regulations: how one entered the classroom, how one greeted the teacher, how one left, how one put away the materials, how and when the lights were clicked off and the doors closed, and so forth. Any student who was absent during roll call was marked absent, and if he or she arrived late, he or she was marked tardy. The elementary school was subjected to a series of time-related penalties (lateness, absences, truancies, cutting), of deportment (inattention, negligence, lack of effort), of behavior (rudeness and insolence), of speech (idle chatter), and of the body (unpleasant hand movements, hostile gestures, poor habits of cleanliness). A cluster of black marks or chastisements were used by teachers, from ridicule to detention and corporal punishments. The departure from preferred behavior and deportment standards was at the center of the disciplinary mechanisms operating in these overcrowded classrooms.

The pupil's offense was not only failure to observe minirules that governed associations in the classroom; it also encompassed inability to perform schoolwork satisfactorily. When a youngster had failed to learn the lesson, he or she was forced to repeat it until it was mastered; either he or she was forced to stay after school, or he or she was given an extra assignment or homework.

School discipline had to enforce a social order that was established by legal-rational authorities, a program that was set forth in a series of general regulations and laws, but in the overcrowded classroom, the one overwhelming and obvious need was order. Time was needed for the children to master a lesson or skill, for a youngster to be examined and placed in his or her proper grade level or ability group. This was to prevent student frustration that might develop if the work was too hard or too easy for them. Levels of efficiency were clearly marked, and students who failed to master the work of a particular grade were often asked to repeat that grade until they did succeed.

School discipline was essentially corrective in nature, as it always had been. The defects of immigrant children were used as reasons for assigning additional work or memorizing certain lessons. Offenses were punished by forcing the student to repeat and duplicate work that was not done in a satisfactory way. Punishment became a mechanism of instruction and training for these children from faraway places.

Of course, the disciplinary system offered rewards as well as punishments, making it part of the corrective regimen of the public school. Gold stars, banners, and special privileges were given to those who performed their schoolwork in exceptional manners. Behaviors were labeled as good or bad rather than simply as acts that were permitted or rejected by teachers. They were recorded and used to develop grades for individual students. What was put in place was a system of rewards based upon the cumulation of acceptable behavior and work. The place of a youngster in the class and his or her abilities in different subjects were identified and placed in rank order next to those of fellow classmates.

Placing students in grades and ranking them helped teachers locate areas of academic weakness and to pinpoint the areas that needed work, but it also stigmatized many while rewarding the few. The rewards of stars, stickers, checks, numerical grades, or commendation certificates were simply the other side of the punishment system. Punishment was often provided by not giving such rewards to youngsters who did not do what they were told and taught to do. The grades, which were also ranked, rewarded some while punishing others, too. At P.S. 122 in Manhattan, different classes were awarded banners for perfect attendance, 100 percent white shirts at assembly time, and high academic achievement test scores. These rewards were given to students on a daily or weekly basis, based on reports of teachers and administrators. The classes of a grade were designated as the first class, the second, and so on. The first was made up of the smartest and best-behaving children in the grade. They, therefore, were usually the ones who received most of the awards. The second-ranked class was good, but not as good as the first. The lesser-ranked classes were made up of low achievers, more poorly behaved students, and the like. They seldom, if ever, won awards. They ware also designated in ways that made their shameful condition obvious to all. Because achievement and deportment alone decided the rank and standing of a youngster, the student was duty-bound to raise the standards of his or her work and classroom behavior. When improved, he or she was given the chance to return to the better, more-productive classes. Often, however, he or she remained mired in classes with fellow failures, behavior did not improve, and he or she dropped out of school at an early age. This method of punishing and rewarding children had a dual effect: students were assigned to classes according to their achievement and conduct while being pressured by teachers to improve their standing by further efforts. Youngsters had to be properly subservient, attentive, and nonthreatening in their gestures and movements.

However, classroom discipline was not concerned with repressing deviant and hostile behavior alone. It compared the acts of students with one another while training them to follow the idea of life lived by a set of rules and regulations. Youngsters were measured by how well they followed those rules and the directions of the teacher. These were sometimes too easy or too difficult for different students. The nature of the student was, thus, determined in quantitative terms over time and ranked according to ability levels. This micropenality of the classroom differentiated students on a day-to-day and moment-to-moment basis. It ranked them, standardized their work, and separated and excluded malcontents and slow learners. It created a normal order from which deviancy could be identified by simple military and penal surveillance techniques.

Micropenality systems were essentially concerned with what happens to children once they enter the classroom and begin to play out the student role. How can they be kept busy and out of trouble? These systems also had a moral as well as social rationale. Discipline, as it developed in these schools, was not only a preventative and security apparatus. It sought, too, to arrange time more rationally so that students and teachers could make better use of it.

It sought also to provide as many moments of learning and moral enlightenment as it could from the school day. This meant that teachers and students were encouraged to intensify their efforts at every moment, to maximize their efficiency and speed in performing their pedagogic and learning tasks. It was precisely these goals of maximum effort and productivity that were enunciated in the factories and workshops that were developing in the United States at this time.

Through these systems of rewards and punishments, these schedules and timetables, these instruments of constraint and suppression, a new type of citizen and worker was being formed. Slowly the students committed themselves to a mechanical performance of schoolwork. The future citizen-worker submitted, finally, to the school's demand that his or her body perform specified tasks in the correct order, at the correct moment in time, and in accordance with the perspectives of the educational staff. In surrendering one's body to the new instruments of organizational dominance, the student received relevant training for future life in the authoritarian workplaces of industrial society. It was the body's ability to perform tasks that was of interest to the school organization, rather than its spiritual or moral qualities. It was the body's way of submitting itself to authority that was of the utmost importance. The physical miracle of the human body was not important here. The training of that body to perform useful labor became the paramount concern of educational and business leaders. In the discipline that was imposed from without, in the resistance that such regimentation aroused, the body learned to reject those behaviors and gestures that were incompatible with the successful completion of its work in the school and workplace.

NOTES

1. Ellwood P. Cubberley, *Public Education in the United States* (Boston, Mass.: Houghton-Mifflin, 1934), pp. 480–84; Selwyn Troen, *The Public and the Schools: Shaping the St. Louis System, 1838–1920* (Columbia: University of Missouri Press, 1975), pp. 205–9.

2. Cubberley, *Public Education in the United States* pp. 285–89; Ellwood P. Cubberley, "The School Situation in San Francisco," *Educational Review* 21 (April 1901): 364–68.

3. Irving Howe, *World of Our Fathers* (New York: Simon and Schuster, 1976), pp. 272–74.

4. Colin Greer, *The Great School Legend* (New York: Basic Books, 1972), pp. 19–20; John E. Craig, "The Expansion of Education," *Review of Research in Education* 9 (1981): 151–213.

5. David Tyack, "Bureaucracy and the Common School: The Example of Portland, Oregon 1851–1913," *American Quarterly* 19 (Fall 1967): 475–98.

6. Tyack, "Bureaucracy in the Common School," pp. 477–78; Lawrence A. Cremin, *American Education: The National Experience, 1783–1876* (New York: Harper & Row, 1980), pp. 24–29.

7. Ellwood P. Cubberley, *Changing Conceptions of Education* (Cambridge, Mass.: Houghton-Mifflin, 1908), pp. 49–52.

8. David Tyack, *Turning Points in American History* (Waltham, Mass.: Blaisdell Publishing, 1967), pp. 315–16.

9. Horace Mann, "Fifth Report of the Secretary Board," *School Reform: Past and Present*, Michael B. Katz (Boston, Mass.: Little, Brown, 1971); Carl E. Kaestle and Maris A. Vinovskis, *Education and Social Change in Nineteenth Century Massachusetts* (Cambridge, Mass.: Cambridge University Press, 1980), pp. 44–49.

10. Michel Foucault, *Discipline and Punishment: The Birth of the Prison* (New York: Pantheon Books, 1977), pp. 190–94.

11. Ibid., pp. 172–74.

12. Michael B. Katz, "The New Departure in Quincy, 1873–1881: The Nature of Nineteenth Century Educational Reform," *The New England Quarterly* 40 (March 1967): 17–20.

13. From my field notes. See also, Timothy L. Smith, "Immigrant Social Aspirations and American Education, 1880–1930," in *Education in American History: Readings on Social Issues* ed. Michael B. Katz (New York: Praeger, 1973), pp. 236–50.

14. Foucault, *Discipline and Punishment*, pp. 149–51, 156–61.

15. Ibid., pp. 177–84.

16. Stanley Rothstein, "The Ethics of Coercion," in *Urban Education* 22 (April 1987): 53–72.

4

Organizational Perspectives

School officials and reformers were overcome, at the end of the nineteenth century, by an impulse to confine urban youth in overcrowded, mass institutions. Everywhere we find the same sense of pride in common schooling, the same mission of moral suasion and acculturation. Schooling was the "common birthright of every American child."[1] Lawrence Cremin, writing of this period, echoed their themes: "common schools increased opportunity, . . . taught morality and citizenship, encouraged a talented leadership, maintained social mobility, (and) promoted responsiveness to social conditions."[2]

The entire period was taken up with efforts to stabilize the future of U.S. democracy. During this period of intense immigration and growing urban poverty, the schools were "the prime essential to good democratic government and national progress," according to Ellwood P. Cubberley.[3] Yet, it was simple enough to show the falsity of these claims. For most of the nineteenth century, an overwhelming number of urban children did not complete their primary grades, and many never attended any school at all.[4]

MASS SCHOOLS IN URBAN SETTINGS

What were the schools like during this period? Those who visited the urban schools of Portland, Oregon, in 1913 recalled with dismay what they had seen. They were depressed by the impersonality and rigid bureaucratic routines; they observed a "prescribed, mechanical system, poorly adapted to the needs either of the children or the community";[5] they saw a completely mechanical and rote system of instruction, where the school's organization, administration, supervision, and procedures were controlled by inspections and examinations. Before Cubberley, before William Torrey Harris, there had been the earlier reformers and Horace Mann; there had been a continuing concern with preserving the existing social order in urban settings; and afterwards, there had been a pressing need to control and manage the lives of urban youth in congested, underfunded, poorly heated schools. A generation after the exclamations of Joseph Rice in St. Louis (1870), we hear again that teachers and students are victims of a faceless, bureaucratic administration. Portland students were being reduced to automatoms: teaching "varied only in so far as it was necessary . . . so that everyone learned exactly the same things in the same way." Everyone was to develop a common body of attitudes and knowledge. All were trained to be as alike as possible in their knowledge and responses to teacher commands.[6]

Bureaucracy was in fashion. It was seen as the most effective way of dealing with the unending demands of urban schooling: poverty and antisocial habits and attitudes were to be suppressed and replaced by a more orderly, productive urban American. It was important, school authorities were saying, to transform the immigrant and urban youth into uniform, obedient future workers. "Americanization required clean hands, regular use of the toothbrush, a balanced diet, patient personal industry, neat dress, and an idyllic middle-class family life."[7] School authorities also said that the teaching of patriotism and a respect for the traditions and customs of the capitalist United States were of the utmost importance. Still earlier in the nineteenth century, there had developed many of the practices that more complex, urban schools demanded: the dependence on more and more specialized personnel; the institutionalization of hierarchies that determined the rank and status of every adult and child along with their degree of prestige, authority, deference, rights, privileges, and salaries; the establishment of communication channels that flowed downward; the obsession with efficiency and the rationalization of school practices so that organizational conflict could be reduced to a minimum; and the imposition of a myriad of rules and regulations that defined who held the decision-making rights inside the school building. Were not these organizational characteristics clearly described by the great German philosopher Georg Wilhelm Friedrich

Hegel in the 1820s? Did William Torrey Harris and others do anything more than codify organizational practices and patterns that were already ascendant in the army, prisons, giant corporations, and state governments? The rapid immigration of eastern and southern Europeans from 1848 to the end of World War I was surely one of the most pressing causes of this rush to accept bureaucratic structures and practices, as was the need to reduce cultural and value differences among the different populations that migrated to the nation's urban centers.

Still, bureaucracy in urban schools did not emerge fully developed. When William Torrey Harris sought to consolidate existing practices, he was simply completing the work that had been begun by Horace Mann. Mann had sought to establish order out of the chaos of urban education by standardizing the methods, content, and materials in common schools.[8] The grading of classes and the training of teachers were to be part of an overall attempt to regulate behaviors, and the results were that urban schooling was made more uniform in the larger towns and cities of the Northeast and West. These successful reforms also established schools that tended to control student behavior further, thus, undermining the original goals of the earliest reformers, who sought to train independent, upright citizens in humane environments. The schools became state agencies that taught certified, predigested ideas and facts and enforced a military discipline upon students. A statement justifying these pedagogic practices can provide us with additional insight into the thinking of school authorities: "the peculiarities of civil society and the political organization draw the child out of the influence of the family nurture"; the school, then, must compensate by emphasizing discipline and by making "far more prominent the moral phase of education."[9] Late in the nineteenth century, there was a demand from immigrants that the public schools of St. Louis be taught in their native tongue; opposition was voiced about the use of textbooks and other pedagogic practices.[10] For William Torrey Harris, the superintendent of schools, the large German population and their demand for German language instruction posed a threat to the entire concept of public schooling in the United States, because the purpose of common schools, if they had any purpose at all, was to transform immigrants into English-speaking Americans.

A graded system of instruction was already in place when Harris assumed his position, and the Board of Education and monetary control were both free of the City Council and other state apparatuses. Yet, it is important to note the differences that transformed a flexible policy of grade promotion into a reward and punishment system that controlled what was taught in every classroom in St. Louis. Harris' policies evolved within the context of an educational movement toward greater efficiency and control that related itself more closely than ever to Administration's need for conformity, control, inspection-oriented supervision, and evaluation. They developed under the protective wing of a more scientific method of ordering urban schools, a more business-like way of providing for observable and accountable learning practices. If it simply formalized existing practices, it did so within the realm of the immediate and pressing needs of school authorities and mass institutions.

One obvious change in the organizational structure of schools was the complete scheduling of pedagogic activities and experiences. The school year itself was divided into quarters of approximately ten weeks each.[11] No promotion, no reclassification was possible until the end of one of these quarters, and an attempt was made to group the good, average, and slow learners for instruction. It was the requirements of the mass, urban schools themselves that seemed to demand these innovations; it was from the need to acculturate and control the bodily movements of huge numbers of students that these bureaucratic practices first received their greatest impetus and acceptance by reformers and school authorities alike.

An administrative triumph of some dimensions was achieved, because if the schools were standardized and graded uniformly, meaningful supervision of instruction could occur: teachers and students could be evaluated and ranked according to their achievements. The principals of these St. Louis schools were chosen by Harris to serve as supervisors for primary schools. Each of them was to visit and observe every school in his area once a week. He was to talk to teachers and administrators, to visit classrooms, and to report to the superintendent on what he had seen. He was to maintain a close contact with pupils and their classrooms and do some teaching as well. Principals, teachers, and students were observed by Harris himself, and endless reports were filed in the central office. A kindergarten was introduced in 1873, and sepa-rate schools with kindergartens were established later in the decade. Students were encouraged to attend classes in order to improve their educational knowledge and skills. Harris was also responsible for professionalizing the teacher preparatory school and adding evening and vocational classes for immigrant students and their families. These adult classes were conducted in German, but Harris continued to insist that the children in public day schools be taught in English. He also insisted that teachers and supervisors grade children more closely; music, drawing, and gymnastics were added to the subjects taught. The more we look at the reforms of this important superintendent, the easier it is to see the general outlines of the modern bureaucratic educational system: increasingly, the methods used to service an immigrant, urban working class student body were accepted by schools across the country in order to meet the demands of ordering and controlling large numbers of youth in congested surroundings. Harris recognized in the overburdened, crowded urban schools both a need to discipline and a need to transform these poor and immigrant children. Here is how he described his schools:

The course of study is laid down with a view to giving the pupil the readiest and most thorough practical command to those conventionalities of intelligence, those arts and acquirements which are the means of directive power and of further self-education. These preliminary educational accomplishments open at once to the mind of the pupil two opposite directions: (a) the immediate mastery over the material world, for the purposes of obtaining food, clothing and shelter directly; (b) the initiation into the means of association with one's fellow-man, the world of humanity.[12]

Superintendent Harris believed that his office was in the process of evolution and change.[13] Earlier, superintendents had been concerned mostly with the administrative tasks of educational systems. Their work was preoccupied with school properties, supply allocations, record keeping, and building maintenance and construction. The change in this office reached into the very heart of the pedagogic process, into the development of courses of study and instructional practices. Superintendents seemed to be ideally placed to inspire schoolteachers while providing the elected or appointed boards of education with expert advice and counsel. Harris believed that the public schools must be a learning community that emphasized the U.S. cultural heritage and language. The core of his efforts were directed toward conserving and transmitting the achievements of the race.

This idea that confinement in a public school necessarily led to acculturation and the transformation of unruly urban youth — was this not similar to the ideas of Horace Mann and the Lancastrian schools of the early nineteenth century? Having to study and work in these bureaucratic structures, amid graded schools, regular examinations, attendance reports, salary schedules, and standardized maintenance and supervision procedures, how could students avoid acquiescing in the shallow relations and institutional identities they were assigned? Harris himself emphasized "order rather than freedom . . . work rather than play, . . . effort rather than interest, . . . prescription rather than election, . . . regularity, silence and industry that 'preserve' and reproduce the civil order."[14] The primitive nature of urban youth was an impediment to their development and freedom in later life. Urban schooling was still thought of as a training and preparation for adulthood: students were to become the well-disciplined work force of an expanding industrial nation.

The administrative apparatus sought to limit the freedom of urban youth during this period, ignoring the psychological effects of mass bureaucratic environments and military discipline. William Torrey Harris' reforms were in the direction of greater efficiency and predictability of teacher and student behavior. Following the rules and regulations was made a demand of school life. The idea of the public school as the societal agency responsible for standardizing pupils and preparing them for life in the industrial United States became widely accepted. Schooling appeared as the transformer and redeemer of urban poor and immigrant youth, who were now seen as a potential threat to the existing order and character of the nation.

Still, confinement in militaristic, bureaucratic schools caused alienation and massive failures: regimentation made students into robots or rebels, and drop-out rates soared. The malfunctioning of these bureaucratic schools was greatest, perhaps, in the urban schools that served the native and immigrant poor; extreme disciplining of bodily movements and thought was experienced there; defeated children were forced to experience degradation and failure; poverty and harsh economic conditions kept most from completing their primary grades. The administration never tired of pointing out the distinctiveness of their poor and foreign-born pupils; it asked that more funds be appropriated to run these ever-expanding bureaucracies; and — it is important to remember — most school authorities suggested that these children needed to be morally and culturally transformed into more uniform and standardized "products."

An organizational rigidity was established to deal with these tasks, a rigidity that separated urban schooling further from the poor and immigrant communities. The Americanization of immigrants and urban poor youth now became a concern of the educational expert and professional. Schooling now appeared with the organizational forms that characterized its nature into our own times. The presence or urban poor and immigrant children appeared to be an intolerable burden to the already overburdened city and state governments. The strange languages and customs had an unsettling effect on the reformers. Schooling was tied, again, to the personal rejection and transformation of the student, to the Americanization of the urban poor and foreigners. This schooling rejected the youngsters as they were and condemned them to authoritarian classrooms that mimicked the workplace. The social rejection and the need to transform students existed in tandem. Together they symbolized the nation's intention to make the newcomers Americans who could easily accept and fit into the factories and bureaucratic workplaces in industrial society. The schools alone were to provide a way for the urban and immigrant poor to raise themselves up. Between the legal demand for compulsory schooling and the social rejection that characterized education's pedagogic practices, a powerful tradition of inculcation was established and maintained.

From all sides there was the demand for a reasoned response to the alien habits and nature of the immigrants, a response that could order and control them and teach them to live by the rules of the school and workplace. The immigrant was a stereotyped, distant figure to many Americans. He was a raw material that could be fashioned into a U.S. role with the proper education. Affluence and social status became linked to education, even though most immigrants entered the middle classes by means of trade and merchandising skills they had brought with them from the Old World.

Ever-increasing pockets of urban poverty and immigration were major forces in shaping the U.S. educational response to these problems. The vast numbers of immigrants made them expendable in the eyes of some. They were a constant source of cheap labor that lowered the costs of production and helped to develop cost-effective bureaucratically organized commerce and industry. In a labor market that contained many unskilled jobs, the schools could fail large numbers of urban youth and still not consign them to an adult life of poverty and unemployment.

Summing up, the armies of urban poor and immigrant youth were an important factor in the educational system's attempts to rationalize the organizational structures of urban schools. The core of this problem seemed to lie in the diverse backgrounds of the immigrants and poor and their perceived threat to Anglo-Saxon culture and traditions. The prejudices against these urban populations mounted steadily and affected the way their children were taught in overcrowded classrooms. That is not in question. Superintendents believed, along with Harris, that confinement and acculturation were essential and beneficial; none of these urban youth should be excluded from the coercive, standardizing experience of schooling; their place was in schools, where they could learn what they would need to know to function well in the world of work.

Why were the urban poor and immigrants willing to accept such an education? Perhaps it was because they believed that once they had been Americanized, their children would have a better life. Those who failed did so because of their own poor efforts and inadequacies, school authorities assured any who would listen. For educators, the shame was not that the urban and immigrant poor failed in their schoolwork but that so many dropped out or failed to attend school at all. How, then, could they substantiate their claim that they helped the impoverished and immigrant to assimilate into U.S. society? They did make this claim, nevertheless, in the face of their own reports documenting their monumental failures.

What triumphed in this period of bureaucratic school reform was not the individualistic, pragmatic philosophy of John Dewey but the scientific, efficiency-oriented methods of bureaucratic structures. Education was suffused with these practices long before William Torrey Harris, not from the rationalist perspective but from the more-pressing demands for military disciplines in mass institutions. Even after the Civil War, urban education was uniformly organized around the requirements of its enormous size; its hierarchy; its preoccupation with rank, status, and authority; and its need to be free of conflict.

Given the responsibility for Americanizing the immigrant and urban youth and forced to do so in the same schools that had failed the immigrant and poor of previous generations, urban education had to deal with the problems of acculturation and equal opportunity as best it could. Harried legislators and reformers, unable to point to what the schools were themselves reporting, began to demand greater accountability. What developed, in the course of these reforms, was not the single, comprehensive curriculum of Horace Mann and the common schoolers but the differentiation of tracks according to ability levels. Meritocracy was set free in the schools long before William Torrey Harris, not from the need to sort out children alone but from an institutional requirement: control of student behavior demanded a military discipline in overcrowded classrooms and buildings. Even before this period, a youth's future was largely determined by his or her level of attainment and that social condition of his or her family.

Standardized, graded for difficulty, and designed to provide uniformity of instruction and outcomes at a low per-pupil cost, meritocracy became a more objective judgment. The stage had been set for the introduction of formal examinations that evaluated and recorded levels of achievement for every student, ranking him or her in a hierarchy of academic success.[15]

THE EXAMINATION SYSTEM

The examination in the public schools served a dual purpose: it allowed teachers and others to observe the levels of student achievement, and it provided a norm for evaluating and ranking that achievement. It was an instrument of stratification, a method of surveillance that made it possible to differentiate, to classify, and to reward or punish. That was why, in the bureaucratic structures of the late nineteenth century, the examination was highly valued by school authorities. In it were found the force and authority of a seemingly fair competition, the discipline of a just and normal evaluation. At its center was the objectification of the student's identity and schoolwork, the transformation of physical and mental abilities into quantitative data that could be more easily managed and digested by the organization's communication system. The imposition of standardized examinations and classroom tests reemphasized the power and standing of teachers in their relations with students (and parents). It was also another way that outside social forces determined what would be taught in every classroom in a given state.

Researchers have written of the effects of textbooks or socioeconomic status on the experience of children in modern schools, but few educators have written about the examination system and its place in the harsh disciplinary system of the common schools. How did these rituals of test taking affect the psychological well-being and self-esteem of students? How did they function as a mechanism of social control and stratification? Who were the persons involved in these constant measurements of student progress? How were questions and answers used to establish uniformity of instruction in diverse classrooms throughout the United States? And, finally, how was the grading of students used to track and classify them, to stream them into the different levels of learning and earning? Because, in the examination system, students and their teachers were forced to accept another's definition of knowledge and worthwhile schoolwork. The myths and ideologies of educators like Edward L. Thorndike and other powerful interests were institutionalized and found their way into all areas of professional instruction and certification in the next century. The examination was also used in hiring people for factories and offices. It was not simply a matter of recalling and showing what an individual student knew but a matter of accepting the authority and knowledge perspectives of those in positions of political power and influence.

One of the primary characteristics of schooling during this period of bureaucratic expansion was the organization of the pedagogic work around these external examinations and standards. In its less-formal mode, this consisted of visits from board members, superintendents, and building administrators. In the standardized classrooms of this era, the superintendent, coming from the central office, added his impressions and demands to the other mechanisms of social control and discipline. The visits to inadequate schools caused principals to become more exacting in their pursuit of district goals. In 1892, Joseph Rice was able to visit 1,200 classrooms in 36 cities. He was able to observe actual lessons in progress and to record his impressions. In most of these classrooms, he found principals who judged the effectiveness of teachers according to how well they followed the prescribed curriculum. That pedagogic approach assumed that "when a child enters upon school life his vocabulary is so small that it is practically worthless."[16] It insisted upon frequent drilling of students until they lapsed into silent and passive drudges and automatons. The supervisory visits of administrators were part of the examination system. The inspections placed teachers in a situation that constantly scrutinized their efforts and forced them to adjust their teaching so that pupils could do well on the formal examinations that measured their academic progress each school year. This had some serious consequences. In the internal structure of the organization, the administrator began to gain control over teachers and to relegate many of them to subordinate roles inside their own classrooms. The role of teacher as drillmaster and martinet established classroom atmospheres that were grim and factorylike. "The unkindly spirit of teachers," spurred by supervisory pressures and the omnipresent examinations, "completely subjugated pupils to the teacher's will." The well-disciplined school became the norm and the model in most cities and towns of the nation. School discipline could now concern itself with more than merely regimenting student movements and gestures. Now, it could focus on enforcing an "arbitrary cult of uniformity" on all aspects of the educational experience of children.[17]

Similarly, the school's recitations and lessons became more concerned with a daily testing and review process that prepared students for the final, formal examinations. It became a routine competition among students and a constant mode of comparison, making it possible for educators and politicians to measure and evaluate individual students objectively. Charles W. Eliot of Harvard believed that teachers saw little or no reason to regard students as conscious persons. "They wanted all the pupils in a given room to be in one grade . . . to move together like soldiers on parade, and to arrive on examination day having all performed precisely the same tasks."[18] Educators and social reformers wanted youngsters to be tested daily and weekly: on Monday for arithmetic, on Tuesday for spelling, on Wednesday for geography, and so on. Moreover, there was to be a formal examination once a month so that a pupil's progress could be determined. Joseph Rice described the consequences of these rigid curriculums and teaching practices for us, echoing the findings of John Goodlad in the 1980s. "In order to reach the desired end, the school has been converted into the most dehumanizing institution that I have ever laid eyes upon, each child being treated as if he possessed a memory and the faculty of speech, but no individuality, no sensibilities, no soul."[19] The examinations did not merely measure the memory and recall of students and signal an end to a certain time in the semester. It was a constant and permanent feature of the schooling experience. It was enmeshed in the discipline system and used as, yet, another instrument of suppression and control of student behavior. The examination guaranteed the authority and standing of the teacher and administrator in their daily work with children. The classroom became the place where children looked to the teacher as the one person who could tell them what was meaningful and important and what was not. It was a continuation of the process of pedagogic institutionalization that had begun with the old charity schools. The triumph of bureaucracy and its examination system marked a moment in time when the educational hierarchy and standardized pedagogic methods became fixed in an unchanging mode.

The examination allowed educators to exercise control over teachers and students even when they were far away from the classroom. It transformed the daily observations and judgments of teachers into a final summing-up, a written and permanent record of test scores that could objectify teacher evaluations of students. What was seen by students was the power of the teacher. She was the force that controlled their movements and guided their efforts and attention during the school day. Those who devised the curriculum and coerced teachers into a slavish acceptance of these new methods were hardly mentioned or seen by pupils, but their influences were deeply felt. Their disciplinary power was exercised through an invisible chain of command. They imposed their ideas on teachers and students by issuing a cascade of memos, directives, and regulations and by mandating certain examinations. In the discipline system, it was the teachers and pupils who needed to be seen and observed by outside mentors! The power over them was assured by their visibility during visits and by the test scores that showed whether they were teaching the correct materials to the children. It was this constant exposure, of always being able to be observed and corrected, that kept children and teachers in their subordinate positions, and the examination was the way in which those in roles of higher authority, instead of dictating directly what should be taught and accomplished, controlled what happened in classrooms across the country. By selecting and ranking students, by sorting and licensing teachers, the bureaucracy exercised disciplinary power over its teachers and students. The examination was the ritual that legitimized the pedagogic efforts of teachers and students, quantifying their academic achievements and making it possible to compare and rank them.

Until this triumph of bureaucracy, the classroom visit maintained the power and dominance of school administrators. It was a tangible example of their superior rank during which they renewed their knowledge and awareness of classroom life. The appearance of the principal brought with it a ritualistic response from teachers and students.[20] Even the follow-up conference occurred with all the force of a teacher evaluation. Discipline, here, had its own ethos and methodology. It was a review of expected behaviors, a parade of preferred activities and methods, a prelude to the examination and end-term evaluation of teachers.

In the eyes of administrators, students were so many units of production that had to be observed and controlled. Administrators did not personally engage students. They dealt only with the numbers and files that represented their achievements and failures in urban classrooms. In St. Louis, Superintendent William Torrey Harris made such supervisory visits in order to determine whether teachers were teaching the facts and obtaining the desired results. Joseph Rice has described these schools in some detail. They worked to prepare students for examinations and used "pure, unadulterated, old-fashioned grind" and drill. On the teacher's command, the students were taught to answer questions in a preselected order, "every recitation being started by the first pupil in the class, the children then answering in turn, until all had recited." On the completion of one student's recitation, the next child in line rose to begin the response to the teacher's question or demand. Each youngster called out answers as quickly as he or she could, screaming "their utterances at the tops of their voices, so that no time was wasted in repeated words inaudibly uttered." In their seats, heads were facing the teacher or the blackboard from "whence wisdom" was supposed to "flow." In the background was the school's maxim: "Save the minutes." The teachers were judged on the basis of the results of their students' examination scores and their ability to teach in the accepted manner while maintaining tight classroom discipline. The children were given "ready-made thoughts" in order to save the minutes required to think though a problem on their own. Students were immobilized in their seats and encouraged to control the movement of their limbs and head. "Why should they look behind when the teacher is in front of them?" one teacher asked during one of Rice's visits. The most remarkable feature of these schools were their "severity of . . . discipline, a discipline that enforced silence, immobility, and mental passivity."[21]

These pedagogic practices were adopted because they helped to transform immigrant and urban youth and because they made it easier to manage and control them in the overcrowded schools of the times. The goal of the classroom instruction was "simply to secure results by drilling the pupils in the facts prescribed for the grade."[22] The visibility of administrators was used as a method for training teachers to succeed in preparing students for their examinations, and it was these examinations that determined the nature of instruction and classroom life.

These examinations also allowed teachers and administrators to document the work of individual students more carefully. They formed a cumulative record of a pupil's deportment and achievement. Students were thrust into a world of constant surveillance and ranked according to their ability to do schoolwork. They were defined in terms of the results of that work and the examinations that came each year. An ability to take and pass tests became an important part of the school's overall disciplinary system. On many points, it was modeled after the methods of classical bureaucracy in ancient China, though with some obvious differences. There was the concern for identifying students, for classifying and describing them. This was an important problem in the overcrowded urban school, where it was necessary to track all students, avoid having youngsters repeat classes unnecessarily, correct information given by teachers, know the level of achievement of each pupil, and establish with some degree of assurance the records of those who succeeded and those who did not. It was necessary to identify students, isolate malcontents and delinquents, follow the sequence of achievement, study the proper placement, and determine career paths in the graded educational system. Aptitudes had to be defined, abilities certified.

Hence the rigid classroom routines and disciplinary acts that sought to homogenize the thoughts and movements of children. The use of the examination determined what kind of information was significant and how it could best be taught, leading, in turn, to coding of performances that formalized the status relationships in classrooms.

The rise of bureaucracy meant that these features of schooling were now accumulated in written documents and used to classify, to categorize, to average, and to fix norms for different grade levels. The keeping of attendance and tardy records, the follow-up procedures, the ways such offenses were transcribed, the use of examination scores to compare, and the transmission of such data to the central office formed a uniformed process by which schools were subjected to a disciplinary regime.

This emphasis on the examination and written records had two consequences. First, the student was constituted as an object of answers that needed to be constantly described and updated in order to ascertain progress and evolution. Second, these mechanisms made possible the measurement of achievement, the delineation of groups of students, the characterization of certain facts collected over time, and the calculation of the grade level differences among youngsters and their places in a ranked order of achievement and deportment.

Today, we are so familiar with these methods of enumeration and notation, of registration, of individual, cumulative files for students, of sorting out and defining information that we fail to see them as part of the disciplinary control system of state schools. However, the emergence of the clinical sciences brought this transformation of the individual into data, this use of a file to make determinations based on accumulated data. The student, surrounded by the documentary demands of bureaucratic organizations and the examination system, was reduced to a "case" that could be disposed of by administrative action. He or she could be summarized, measured by achievement scores, judged according to deportment, compared with other children, and placed according to "ability level." He or she could be scheduled for further training or corrective classes, classified, and placed in suitable slots in the organizational structure.

The personal identity of the child was, thus, remade into an institutional one, often quite different from the way he or she was perceived by families and friends. To be examined, observed, described, and recorded was a comparatively new phenomenon in the history of human associations and organizational life. The representations and dispositions of students in this system were a form of subtle domination and control. The transformation of real persons into organizational data was a procedure of discipline. It forced children to subject themselves to adult scrutiny and control in the name of objective examinations. They were labeled as superior or inferior persons in classrooms based on their ability to do schoolwork. The marks that teachers gave students became a symbol of power, giving youth their rank and status when they reached the higher levels of learning and earning.

In summary, the examination system was a method that made the student an object that could be more easily manipulated by educators. It combined the surveillance of the supervisory and teaching staff with standardized, uniform learning experiences, facilitating the functions of social and educational stratification assigned to the schools. Its presence forced teachers to make the most of the time they had with students in the classroom. Thus, individual differences became apparent against a background of memorized facts taught in rote fashion and regimenting deportment standards. Teachers did what they could to secure student test scores that reflected well on their pedagogic efforts. "Since nothing, as a rule, tells so well at an examination as a knowledge of facts, — mental power and moral strength being incapable of exact measurement, — it [became] the sole aim of the teacher to load the memory of her pupils with facts." The teacher's ability was "judged by the number of facts which her pupils retained and she therefore spent all her time in crowding the memory of her pupils with facts."[23]

Critics were quick to point out that this type of pedagogic work was merely teaching to tests. They urged a more enlightened approach that allowed students to study real objects in activity-based curriculums that were more interesting and relevant to the children in schools. However, educators believed that allowing youngsters to study real objects was wasteful and that students could learn more quickly by words alone. Thinking required time and space, two commodities that were sadly lacking in these overcrowded urban schools. Reading became a rote recitation of printed words, arithmetic "the art of computing numbers without regard for the relation of things to one another, and the social and physical sciences became merely a clump of data and texts that required memorization and regurgitated responses."[24]

The examinations fixed the purposes of educational training once and for all. Educators were to look for results that could be observed in classrooms where children were rendered motionless, "the room as still as a grave." They were to look, also, at written tests and examinations. The authority of the principals was increased in this system, as was that of superintendents and boards of education. The teacher was put into the role of martinet and drillmaster as never before, with little power to decide things in her own classroom.[25] In this way, the schools reproduced the social relations that existed in schools and in the society that funded the schools. It reproduced the social status and economic conditions of families by passing on their rank and status to their children.

It was a somewhat somber training that did succeed in accomplishing its goals. The schools prepared youth to accept the economic system and the forms of organizational discipline that existed in schools and society as normal ones, as natural structures in an industrial democracy.

NOTES

1. Colin Greer, *The Great School Legend* (New York: Basic Books, 1972), pp. 13–22; Diane Ravitch, *The Great School Wars* (New York: Basic Books, 1974), pp. 65–69.

2. Lawrence Cremin, *The Transformation of the School* (New York: Knopf, 1961), pp. 3–22.

3. Ellwood P. Cubberley, *Public Education in the United States* (Boston, Mass.: Houghton-Mifflin, 1919), pp. 14–17.

4. Howard R. Bowen, *Investment in Learning* (San Francisco, Calif.: Jossey-Bass Publishers, 1977), pp. 339–40; Mary Herrick, *The Chicago Schools: A Social and Political History* (Beverly Hills, Calif.: Sage, 1971), pp. 105–9.

5. Joseph M. Rice, *The Public School System of the United States* (New York: Century, 1893), pp. 30–39.

6. Ellwood P. Cubberley, *The Portland Survey: A Textbook on City School Administration* (New York: World Book, 1916), pp. 125–34.

7. David Tyack, *Turning Points in American Educational History* (Waltham, Mass.: Blaisdell Publishing, 1967), p. 229.

8. Tyack, *Turning Points*, pp. 314–15.

9. Ibid., pp. 315–17.

10. Rice, *The Public School System of the United States*, p. 19.

11. Cremin, *The Transformation of the School*, p. 19.

12. Tyack, *Turning Points*, pp. 324–28; Marvin Lazerson, *Origins of the Urban School: Public Education in Massachusetts 1870–1915* (Cambridge, Mass.: Harvard University Press, 1971), chap. 2–4.

13. Robert Hummel and John Nagel, *Urban Education in America* (New York: Oxford University Press, 1973), pp. 31–36.

14. Cremin, *The Transformation of the School*, pp. 18–21.

15. Greer, *The Great School Legend*, pp. 130–45.

16. Tyack, *Turning Points*, pp. 314–15; see Willard Waller, *The Sociology of Teaching* (New York: Russell & Russell, 1932) for similar descriptions of classroom life.

17. Tyack, *Turning Points*, pp. 315–17.

18. Ibid., p. 316; see also Melvin Kohn, *Childhood and Conformity* (Homewood,

Ill.: Doresy Press, 1969) for an interesting discussion of schooling and its role in compelling conformity on children.

19. Rice, *The Public School System of the United States*, pp. 93–98.

20. Tyack, *Turning Points*, p. 315.

21. Ibid., p. 329; see Orville Brim, *American Beliefs and Attitudes about Intelligence* (New York: Russell Sage Foundation, 1969) to see how completely the examination system has triumphed in the minds of modern Americans.

22. Rice, *The Public School System of the United States*, pp. 97–99.

23. Ibid., pp. 102–5; see Marshall H. Brenner, "The Use of High School Data to Predict Work Performance," *Journal of Applied Psychology* 52 (January 1968): 114–17 to see how educational evaluations are related to future work performances.

24. Richard J. Altenbaugh, "Teachers and the Workplace," *Urban Education* 21 (January 1987): 365–89.

25. Tyack, *Turning Points*, pp. 316–17.

5

The Birth of Modern Schools

The ideas and pedagogic practices of John Dewey and his activity school are well-known to students of education. Their purpose, perhaps, was to recall a golden age when scholars and teachers worked together to establish a child-centered, activity-based, scientifically validated schooling experience for students.

Behind these cooperative efforts, there was a determined attempt to answer important questions about the learning process and the role that manual work, personal experiences, and activities played in the educational development of children. If the spirit of inquiry was to be encouraged in this elite, private university school, it was necessary to link the child's experiences to the forces that were operating in his or her everyday life outside school.

THE ACTIVITY SCHOOL: JOHN DEWEY
AND EDWARD THORNDIKE

This experimental educational institution was an integral part of the University of Chicago from 1896 to 1904, opening its first session with 16 students and two instructors. It was not visions of the mass public school that it suggested but, rather, an informal learning center. It was a place where carpentry, cooking, sewing, and weaving were used to introduce students to the science and geography underlying these forms of human activity. No opportunity was missed to emphasize the link that existed between the schoolwork and the sense of order, discipline, and morality that developed naturally from these vocational operations.[1]

As for the criticism of traditional schools that these practices implied, the story was by now a familiar one. The separation of the public school and its work from the life of its students was an unnatural and unproductive practice. The codifying of knowledge into discrete formal symbols that seemed to replace the actual objects or experiences they sought to describe caused confusion and failure in large numbers of otherwise intelligent students. Dewey adamantly insisted that curriculum that depended upon textbooks and workbooks instead of firsthand experiences caused youngsters to suffer passively through boring lessons and taught them to be overly subordinate and dependent. Students were forced to submit to regimentation and a constant restraint of their thoughts and movements. The insistent theme in all this was Dewey's emphasis on actual experience as the core and content of enlightened curriculum development in child-centered schools. The university school sought to develop a closer relationship between the lessons children learned in school and the lives they led in their homes and neighborhoods. Dewey believed that the gap between these two sets of experiences had to be bridged. He asked that the school develop the same student interest in schoolwork that youngsters regularly displayed in their play and chores at home. As an example, he sought to teach history, science, and art in terms of the experiences, understandings, and values of the individual students. It was imperative that these subjects be made more important in the eyes of the child. Teaching skills and knowledge as an outgrowth of the youngster's level of understanding and achievement meant that schoolwork could become intellectually and emotionally satisfying experiences.[2] As it was, 75 to 80 percent of the child's first years in public schools were spent in learning and mastering symbols without ever relating them to ongoing life experiences.

These, then, were some of the ideas and practices, at least as far as most educators were aware of them: the objective focus on the child, where the learning process and the nature of education could be most easily observed; the firm insistence of Dewey, who wondered aloud how the child could be given classroom experiences that helped him or her to make sense of his or her world; the insights of outstanding psychologists, philosophers, and teachers who were able to see how firsthand acquaintance with the real world could deepen the student's sense of history, society, and art. These images affected schools of education, in one way or another, far into the twentieth century.

The work of John Dewey should be compared with that of Edward Thorndike, one of his later, contemporary reformers. Dewey's work became shrouded in esotericism and mythology during his long lifetime. Thorndike's pseudoscientific approaches were widely accepted and formed the basis for the authoritarian schools that developed across the country.

Dewey's work must be mentioned first. Because it preceded Thorndike's, because he was known to be steeped in philosophy, his work was regarded as an act of scholarship that could not be easily transposed into everyday practice in overcrowded public schools of the time. The truth of these assertions became more apparent as time passed, and the work of Dewey was widely but incorrectly interpreted by critics and proponents alike. Still, the work of both these men accepted the arbitrary nature of educational pedagogy while attempting to make it more scientific and effective. Beneath their apparent differences there was this common acceptance of the pedagogic authority of schools to teach an arbitrary language and culture to poor and immigrant children. They argued only over how this could best be accomplished.

Yet, the questions Dewey raised were significant then and now. How could the mastering of reading, writing, and science be gained while using other subjects as curriculum area background?[3] The truth was that the child could be made to see the methods of study used in schools as useful and appealing processes only if they were somehow related to his or her everyday existence. This perspective could be developed when a student felt a need to gain an expertise and a capacity in a particular area of instruction. Often, alerting youngsters to the reason for acquiring skills was enough to insure their interest and application. The use of books would serve as an instrument of learning, but this would be a learning that sought to evolve from the needs and motivations of the students themselves, and this led to other conclusions. The teaching of reading, as an example, was for each pupil a personal experience that was not to begin until the youngster expressed a desire or a need to gain this skill. Otherwise, it caused undue strain on the eyes and emotions and made it difficult for children to learn other subjects as well. The principal justification for these approaches was this: children would be able to acquire this skill in reading with much less difficulty and with greater efficiency and ease at a later period in their physical and mental development. Reading was taught in the tasks that developed in science and history. It was never thought of as a subject of and by itself. To encourage students to use texts, as was done in the public schools, was to subject children to twin evils.[4] In the curriculum of public schools where uniformity and regimentation went hand in hand, children came to depend on their textbooks as the only way of learning. They were forced to assume passive attitudes and to absorb what was presented to them by pedagogic authorities. Texts forced youngsters to do the same work at the same time, thus, making texts a more desirable method of instruction in overcrowded classrooms. There, the behavioral models and important information were imposed from without in such a way that inquiry was stifled and, often, eliminated.

At the Dewey school, individual attention was provided by using small numbers of children and large numbers of adults and teachers. An attempt was made to work out a systematic curriculum for each child. "Progressive education" had a meaning then: it attempted not to inculcate an arbitrary language and culture but to place pedagogic work on a more scientific basis where it could be validated by the observed laws of nature and child development.

The spectre of punishment, always in evidence in public schools, was thought to be inappropriate in these new settings. Fear and anxiety were reduced to a minimum. However, such feelings must have existed. Those who wrote and studied this school failed to leave any account of such emotional dislocations. If they existed, they must have lived in some zone between competition as it was practiced in the larger culture and cooperation as it was advocated in this private school environment.

John Dewey wrote that boys and girls were treated alike in the school. When students entered the building, they were all assigned to cooking, sewing, and carpentry, besides doing tasks with paper and pasteboard. They wore work clothes, and their tasks were to gain insight into the development and growth of various inventions and social situations. No sooner had they begun their schoolwork than great emphasis was laid upon the relations between humanity and nature. They were taught to see the modes of development in food gathering, habitation, shelter, clothing and industrial technology, and work roles. The younger children began their schoolwork with occupations they could observe at home and in their neighborhoods.[5] At the beginning of the year, students were taught about the occupations in the home. Here, familiarity was addressed to the student directly, not by merely reading about such work but by performing it. The question was not of limiting the learning to the tasks themselves but of identifying and exploring each area of everyday life in order to trace its progression from olden times to the present. The process of abstraction was, thus, shifted to a more natural mode. The student, as a human being possessed of reason and consciousness, was no longer to be the passive recipient of predigested knowledge and insights. The rote remembrance of unrelated facts was no longer the governing feature in the relations between the student and the teacher. Instead, a more concrete form of joint exploration was used to encourage students to take greater responsibility for their academic progress.

We must, therefore, revise the meanings assigned to Dewey's work. Emancipation of the students, abolition of military discipline and bodily restraints, development of an environment in harmony with a scientific and human spirit — these were based in an educational philosophy that was essentially elitist in nature. The real picture was quite different. In fact, Dewey established a school where the overt coercions of discipline were replaced by an ambiguous assignation of responsibility to the manipulated children themselves. Apprehension over conformist behavior no longer preoccupied most children. It persisted, however, in the individual consciousness of the students. The responsibility for learning was transferred to the children, or so it seemed at first glance. Actually, Dewey advocated a subtle and constant manipulation of experience that made a sham of his supposed individualized curriculum. The Dewey school no longer punished the student for ignorance and unworthiness, it is true. But it organized the students' anxieties and apprehensions in a new and powerful way. It made youngsters more aware of themselves and their relations with teachers. It organized a psychologistic method that sought to explain and govern the child's learning in group settings. In other words, by this freedom the student became an object of subtle correction and competition that was not openly sanctioned or recognized by teachers. Also, from the acknowledgement of their responsibilities as originators and students of everyday experiences, the students were asked to operate as supposedly free and responsible adults. This method of education was later used in truncated form in public schools for brief moments and with little success.

Let us not forget that we are in the world of positivistic, pragmatic philosophy, where men can rationalize and improve their condition at will. Occupations came first in the school because of their moral power and their relevancy for youngsters and society alike. In itself, work possessed an inner constraining force superior to all forms of military or penal discipline. It required social relations about which Karl Marx had spoken and the obligation to produce a credible educational outcome. Regular, routinized schoolwork were the most generally effective way to achieve discipline and cohesiveness in mass schools. The work activities in the Dewey school gave students the illusion of freedom to move about as they pleased. That was certainly one of the most agreeable aspects of the progressive method, even though it was ignored in public schools.

Through work, students returned to the methods of order and control of an earlier period. They submitted to a perspective that accepted these occupations and the social and economic power behind them.

Even more powerful than the discipline that sprang from work and group structures were what Dewey called the controlling power of the group process. This focus of social control tended to use social approval as a mechanism of domination, to psychologize and socialize much of the student's work and relationships in school. It gave the pedagogic acts a seemingly pragmatic genuineness that was in tune with the scientific and industrial thinking of the times. In the experimental school, the student was open to observation that measured responses to group life. The child was provided with a new ethos that sought to connect schoolwork with his or her outside existence. The view Dewey now expounded for public education in this period was one of the important contributions he made to school theory. It stated that public schools were one of the main remedies for the dislocations of industrial society. Dewey organized his experimental school's work so as to establish in miniature the world of work as it existed at the turn of the century. There was an obvious need to establish greater social control and efficiency in the schools and factories of the nation, where everyone had to speak a common language and work for the common welfare. Nothing else was to be the goal of public schools except this need to increase social harmony through learnings that emphasized the assimilation needs of U.S. society. The staff of the experimental school, thus, regularly involved students not merely in learning but in "play construction, use of tools, contact with nature, expression, and activity." The school became a place where youngsters were actively engaged in work together rather than in listening to a continuously talking teacher. Students learned about the world in which they lived by inquiring about the nature of origins and cultural differences. The best staff was assembled to teach this elite group of private school students, and the researchers included some renowned psychologists and social scientists. It rarely happened that any unpleasantness occurred, if we can believe the accounts of observers and teachers. Students controlled their negative impulses, and the scenes at the school were at once industrious and affable. These practices sought to simplify modern life so that children could more readily understand its workings. It was the organization around the simple experiences of the children that introduced students, more and more, to the nature of their own world. Incessantly cast in the role of the cooperative and helpful team player and challenged to negate and ignore the attitudes of his or her first pedagogic learnings and culture at home, the student was obliged to remodel himself or herself as the prototype of a more efficient social and industrial citizen. The discipline of activity welcomed the student only with this proviso and at the price of unlearning past experiences and ignoring ambivalent emotional attitudes.

The suppression of physical coercion was part of a system whose essence was that of group control and solidarity. The student's freedom, engaged by activities and group projects and the observations of researchers and teachers, was limited by the will and aspirations of the group. Instead of establishing a simple environment in which a handful of privileged students could explore their interests and concerns freely, "a carefully planned group context" provided youngsters with a "sequence of experiences, which, despite their apparent spontaneity, were in fact meticulously elicited and manipulated by teachers."[6] A transformation from a world of authoritarian discipline to a world of group and staff censure and approval took place. A pedagogy of action would lead children into habits and thoughts that were conducive to the demands of industrial society and democratic governance. Thus, a pedagogy of education became possible, for under scientific scrutiny, all schools were required to reproduce the relationships and culture of the society that established them as legitimate agencies of instruction. All schools were judged only by their outcomes. Few were truly concerned with the intentions of children. Education was responsible for inculcating in youngsters a conformist way of thinking and behaving. All the inner inclinations of children were to be subordinated to the needs of the group and the larger machine culture. The science of education as it developed in Dewey's school, was still concerned with ranking and classifying student progress. The activities were never a free exchange of ideas among equals. This could not be as long as Dewey was so conscious of the need for social control mechanisms in the urban areas and industrial workplaces of the United States. Dewey saw a pressing need to acclimate immigrants and workers to the rigors and hardships of their work. He emphasized the need for instructing assembly-line workers so that they could understand the important role their work played in the new production methods of modern society.

However, Dewey's work had surprisingly little influence on schooling in the urban United States.[7] Perhaps this was because he failed to translate his pragmatic philosophy into useful educational practices in public schools. This was partly because of the bureaucracy's ability to transform suggestions for reform into mere verbal or written communications. Bogged down in "educationese" and the insistent demands of schooling the immigrant and urban poor, progressive practices soon became unrecognizable. The ideas seemed more suited to small, elitist schools. Dewey's more radical ideas were also ignored and praised in the same moment by conservative institutions of higher learning. The public schools continued to be the very opposite of what Dewey advocated during his long lifetime. The stressed passive learning in overcrowded classrooms focused the teacher's attentions on problems of order and control. The needs of the autocratic workplace remained paramount in their calculations, and the needs of a democratic society remained unserved.

Educators mouthed the words of John Dewey while following in their pedagogic efforts the teachings of Edward Thorndike. Dewey had only eight years of actual classroom experience in an unusual, elitist setting. He wrote of the philosophy and psychology of learning in a private school environment. Thorndike essayed and published the dictionaries, texts, and manuals teachers used in their actual everyday teaching. He published many books and materials and trained thousands of teachers to function in the mass schools of the industrial United States.

Surveillance and scientific evaluation were the catchwords of Thorndike and his followers. Already the appearance of his scales of academic achievement were in wide use in schools throughout the country. Thorndike himself suggested this as a way of controlling what was taught in classrooms. Schools could more easily evaluate and standardize their offerings in this way. Something had been added to this embrace of traditional methods of instruction: science. Until the coming of Thorndike, the world of public schooling was evaluated by tests and teacher judgments that were not validated by scientific rationales or methods. The methods were almost always based on traditional forms of authority, in a Weberian sense, even though they were justified by legal-rational mandates from the state. Thorndike established a pseudo-scientific rationale for his work. The agencies authorized by the state to school the young would now be further legitimated by the prestige of the scientific method. Schools would continue to be as they were; they would continue to be modeled after large industrial and military organizations. The standardized test would be the equitable and objective way of classifying and ranking students more effectively.[8] Thorndike and his followers advanced upon public education with a battery of tests and measurements that deeply influenced and solidified the educational and business methods of the status quo. It was not with an arbitrary test of linguistic and cultural understandings that he confronted school children. His standardized tests were fair, unbiased, and scientifically validated. They measured the academic worthiness of students and ranked their accomplishments. Science's victory over the forces of ignorance was once more assured by these objective measurements.

Thorndike had been chairman of the Committee on Classification of Personnel of the Army during World War I and was able to show how group intelligence tests could be used in mass organizations. The implications for inculcation and social stratification were immediately grasped by political and educational leaders. Later, Thorndike was instrumental in developing a National Intelligence Test. He was convinced that intelligence changed little over a person's lifetime and that heredity, not environment, was the dominant variable. The providing of quality education for the lower classes was not as important as providing special courses for gifted children, in his view. He opposed the constant extension of compulsory attendance laws because they falsely raised the hopes of youngsters above their natural abilities and social stations and caused frustration and resentment. Thorndike believed there was a natural order of innate intelligence and that the social and educational stratification of U.S. society could best be accomplished by the statistical ranking of individuals taking common, scientifically standardized tests. His intelligence tests were used to limit the social and educational mobility of immigrant and urban youth and of the poor especially. Those who followed Thorndike mistook wealth for virtue and believed that intellect and character were positively correlated with moneymaking and material success. Thorndike's view that heredity was the primary source of a person's ability had strong racist overtones. He wrote that "racial differences in original nature are not mere myths." Negro children were inferior to whites in scholarship. Their environments were not significant enough to account for the variances in student achievement that were discovered by the tests and measurements Thorndike used.

Of course, all this was in harmony with the movement of teachers, administrators, and others who sought to rank students objectively and to standardize curriculum and teaching methods in overcrowded schools. The standards were "based on white, Protestant, middle class values" and assured Thorndike and his followers of a favorable reaction from educators and the growing middle classes. Thorndike dared to advocate the middle class prejudices of his time and to call them scientific. His work said precisely what the schools and their middle class constituents wanted to hear about themselves and their educational system. Findings of positive correlations between morality, wealth, intelligence, and social power made him the spokesman and darling of the establishment. His notions that "abler persons in the world . . . are more clean, decent, just and kind" cast grave doubt on the quality of his empirical research. These attitudes were age-old and already firmly entrenched in the ideology of the schools. However, now they were clothed in a scientific theory that asserted that "morality, wealth, social power, and cultural advantage" came to those who possessed the char-- acteristics of "racial superiority, intelligence, and real achievement."[9]

FACTORIES FOR FAILURE

The urban school, in its somber austerity, was denounced by only a few. Perhaps this was because the history and nature of these state institutions were still so shrouded in mythology. Perhaps observers could not see the social rejection and assault on the self that accom- panied the pedagogy of acculturation and transformation. They did not see, also, the legions of failures who remained uncounted in the statistical surveys the schools provided on an annual basis for the public. The constant cries of reform seemed to end always in a strengthening of the methods and procedures of bureaucratic discipline and instruction. Then a new innovation was suggested and implemented without the benefit of any research or scientific rationale. Finally, the success or failure of the new reform was judged and integrated into the existing structures or discarded. There was a mechanism of bureaucratic cooption that incorporated innovations into existing practices. The needs of a new, mass educational system required standardized curriculums whose arbitrary nature and language were not easily resisted or understood by teachers or their clients. Reforms that sought to focus the attention of educators on the needs of the children themselves never really took hold in U.S. schools.

One thing seemed apparent at an early period: mass schools did not educate immigrant and poor children effectively. They could force more children to attend for longer periods of time; yet, the rate of their self- confessed failures was astounding. In Chicago in 1898, the schools reported that only 60 percent of the students attending school were at "normal age" grade level. The means of education seemed to be at the disposal of the children of Chicago — the buildings, classrooms, teachers, and supplies were all there. Yet, the numbers of failing students were unacceptably high.[10] Also, the number of those who were no longer survivors, the number of drop-outs, was not reported in this or other reports!

Urban schooling of immigrant and poor children caused the failure rates to soar. Those dropping out of school had little chance to resume their studies later in their lives. Students who stayed in school were forced to endure varying degrees of frustration and failure. Of those who remained in schools, 40 percent were listed as below "normal age" levels in Boston, Chicago, Detroit, Philadelphia, Pittsburgh, New York, and Minneapolis. In Pittsburgh, 51 percent of the students were below "normal age" levels. In Minneapolis, the number of children failing rose to 65 percent! Between 1898 and 1917, the schools continued to issue yearly reports showing that more children were failing in school than were succeeding there. (Of course, these reports asked the public to view the work of survivors only.) As late as 1989 and into the 1990s, New York was reporting that 75 percent of their African-American students were failing, while Texas and California were reporting failure rates among Hispanic students at between 41 and 55 percent!

These failures caused educators in the early part of this century to seek more stringent compulsory education laws. Those urban schools failing immigrant and poor children in such amazing numbers wanted to change the school-leaving age from 12 to 14; later, they sought to change it to 16. Students were kept in school and off the streets for a longer time so they would not inundate the already unsteady labor market. The problems of urban schools were shifted from a concern with student failure to the problem of getting more youngsters into the classrooms and out of trouble. In 1919, 10 thousand work permits were issued to youngsters in Chicago; in 1930, that city granted only 987.[11] Instead of holding back slow learners, the urban schools began to pass them upward. A steady tide of youngsters who had failed in the lower grades now entered secondary schools. They were retained there because of "vanishing opportunities of employment" and the onset of massive unemployment throughout the world during the Great Depression. As late as 1931, George Strayer was acknowledging "that very high failure rates" were "still characteristic" of a majority of public school systems.

The urban schools could not fail to produce large numbers of drop-outs, because of the very type of education they imposed on students. Whether they were compelled to memorize facts or perform endless tasks of drill and rote learning and recitation, from which there was no appeal and no end, it was, in the final analysis, a process that focused not on the youth but on the arbitrary pedagogy and culture that had to be mastered. It was a schooling that established an artificial, unreal world where the student's previous identities and learnings were irrelevant.

The urban schools were given the task of educating youth but in ways that were opposed to their normal physical and mental development. By imposing military discipline, the schools produced armies of truants and delinquents. They were supposed to teach respect for law and order, but their practices caused youngsters to fall behind and drop out at an early age. The reformers continued to insist on compulsory attendance for longer periods of time, pushing the failure rates into the upper grades throughout the 1920s and 1930s. Chicago reported "a sixty-five percent increase among the underprivileged" as late as 1931. At the elementary level, retardation was reported at 61.04 percent of the total student population of survivors, and "forty-one percent of all these entering ninth grade" were seriously behind, too. In tenth grade the figure was 32 percent, but the numbers of drop-outs was high and remained uncounted. Feeblemindedness, overcrowding, and the poor family background of students were given as reasons for these high rates of failure, which were duplicated in Boston, New York, Philadelphia, Detroit, and Washington, D.C. Of the students, 13,000 studied in schools that were on half-day sessions. As late as 1925, 60 percent were "inadequately housed" in schools. Why were the students herded into these congested buildings? In the first two decades of the twentieth century, the students were mostly the children and grandchildren of immigrants and the ever-expanding urban poor. Education for acculturation and the needs of the industrial labor market gave urban schools two compelling reasons for expanding their services in spite of their past failures. As late as 1917, financial pressures on public schools "was so great that urban school systems were actually facing a total suspension of activities."

The urban school made possible the identification of groups of failures and delinquents. Truancy and academic retardation were noted in the survey reports of school districts and recorded in the individual cumulative files of students. Schools organized classes of 30, 40, 50, and more that were then divided into ability groups, ability classes, and so on, and this system of military discipline and evaluation was copied and reproduced across the continental United States.

The unequal competition to which the students were subjected condemned many of them to failure. Their bodily movements were under constant scrutiny and control. They were assigned to certain neighborhood schools and classes that were tracked for failure. The left school without the credentials they needed to show prospective employers. Being poor, being unable to speak English fluently, and leading the life of the foreign-born were the most frequently cited reasons for "high truancy rates and inadequate learning" among the immigrant and urban poor youth. The study committee of a 1911–13 evaluation of the New York City school system "confirmed the relationship between foreign background and poor school performance."[12]

Ultimately, the schools indirectly exacerbated the very delinquency and crime they sought to reduce by throwing youngsters into a labor market without the proper training or credentials. The same act that forced children out of urban schools sent them into an adult world that often seemed harsh and incomprehensible to them. It was in this way that delinquency was furthered by the selection processes of urban educational systems.

Criticisms of these urban schools usually took two lines of response. Some believed that the schools were overly corrective and that the military discipline was crushing the mind and spirit of children. Others felt that attempting to transform immigrant and poor youngsters forced them to experience social and cultural rejection of themselves and their families. In this way, urban schools seemed to be an economic catastrophe. By their ever-increasing costs, they strained the tax base of local communities, and by their failure to root out delinquency and crime, they increased further the costs of local and state government. The responses to these criticisms were always the same. School officials reaffirmed themselves as the primary mechanism for training and controlling youth in a pluralistic, amoral society. For more than a century, the school had been offered as a bulwark against increasing levels of crime and poverty. The revitalization of the common schools was the only means of overcoming these twin afflictions. It was the only way that corrective methods could be applied to the legions of poor and foreign-born that were migrating to the United States.

These ideas were supported by the census of 1900, which showed "one million two hundred and fifty thousand of New York City's three million five hundred thousand inhabitants were foreign born." Of the public school enrollment, 85 percent was made up of foreign-born children. Reformers preached that the schools had to return to their fundamental principles if these newcomers were to be effectively assimilated into the U.S. mainstream.

The pedagogic composition underlying these basic principles was clearly articulated by educators and political leaders of reform at the turn of the century. Compulsory schooling must have as its essential goal the Americanization of the foreign-born. "The great equalizer of the conditions of men" lay in a common school education. Yet, the schools of this period were uniformly overcrowded and congested; half-time and part-time classes and truancy were continuously reported by educators themselves. Students must be placed in grades according to their ages, achievement levels, deportment, and stage of moral and patriotic development. Educators must be given the right to alter established curriculums in order to take account of the disadvantaged condition of students. The progress of youngsters who were severely retarded had to be taken into account when evaluating a district's performance. Because a cardinal principle of the system was the transformation of the student, it was important that students be kept in school as long as possible. A standard curriculum was applied to all with a view toward training youngsters to see the world though the eyes and language patterns of their mentors. These pedagogic efforts included the history and workings of U.S. government and the use and appreciation of the English language. The reward for good conduct and proficiency in schoolwork was the diploma, a document that certified success and opened up employment in better lines of work. Drill must be one of the fundamental means of transforming students into compliant, useful workers and citizens. Drill and rote recitations must be thought of as training in important knowledges and skills and the proper use of time and effort. It must prepare students to heed the instructions of teachers and to do routine, monotonous work with diligence and effort. Every pupil was obliged to be punctual and to memorize and practice lessons and materials. No youngster was allowed to remain idle in the classroom. The principle of continuous activity and work was strictly enforced.

The education of the urban and immigrant poor was both a societal effort and a pressing need. It was in the vanguard of the struggle to rid the nation of crime and poverty, to socialize youth into the U.S. mold. Yet, the schools served to remind the poor of their impoverished condition. "School rooms stank . . . they were ill lit and ill ventilated . . . and rat infested."[13] The educational training of students was focused upon their presumed future status and role in industrial society. The principle of student tracking was in place early in the nineteenth century and remained secure throughout the common school experience. "Americanization always meant making the 'other races' accept the promises and style of the dominant Protestant culture with the clearest white image of itself."

Also, the public schools had to be led and operated by a professional staff possessing an expertise in moral and educational science. This staff was to possess a pedagogic capability that was beyond questioning. Its arbitrary actions and content were to be accepted as being in the best interests of the children and the nation.

Finally, compulsory schooling must be followed by modes of instruction that seek to transform the student from a wild and slothful youth into a docile worker, from a lazy and easily led person into a more useful and functional one, and from a speaker of strange, exotic tongues into an American who spoke and appreciated the virtues of English. Not only must his or her progress through the grade system be certified by documents and diplomas, but also these files must be used to provide him or her with further guidance and assistance.

Again and again, throughout the nineteenth century, the same basic principles or beliefs were repeated in different educational experiences and circumstances. They triumphed anew with each successive attempt to reform the system. The same goals could have been enunciated by the early charity schools. The common schoolers of the mid nineteenth century and the movement toward greater uniformity in pedagogic methods assumed a correct form of language and knowledge acquisition, a superior cultural and linguistic heritage that had to be mastered. At the core of this state schooling apparatus was the feature of military discipline, a type used in mass urban institutions of every kind. A second basic feature was the enormous number of students who were labeled as failures by schools that were supposed to eliminate social inequality. The inefficiency of public schooling was accepted and allowed to continue because it served the needs of a stratified, industrial nation and because it was considered a fair and equitable way of sorting out the deserving from the less deserving citizens. The constant call for reform that characterized the entire history of schooling and its failure to make significant inroads into the nature and character of the system made everyone aware of the change-resistant nature of the state's educational bureaucracy. Reform was part of a process that gave added legitimacy to educators and their work while changing little in the way things were actually done inside the bounded schools themselves.

Of course, the schools were always more than the sum of their pedagogic practices, their fences and gates, their quasiprofessional staffs, and their punishment systems. The system contained within itself symbolic methods of violence and control and architectures, rewards and role definitions, significant social procedures for correcting and transforming youth, and so on. Can we not say, then, that the failure of these schools was part of their function of social selection and stratification? Can we not include these failures as evidence of the effect that military discipline, punishment, and arbitrary pedagogic efforts had on children? Practices in the overcrowded schools were consistently supported in the adult world because they prepared youth for their future roles in the labor market. If schools survived with so little change in their methods or goals, if the idea of compulsory education in mass institutions has seldom been effectively challenged, is it because such systems are very much in harmony with the need and values of U.S. workplaces?

If the schools were to correct and transform immigrant and urban poor children and if they were the primary agency for this inculcation, then failure was to be expected. The level of educational achievement from 1890 onward was one of dismal failure accompanied by requests for more resources and a maintenance of the status quo. The reforms were given lip service when they occurred at all, and the schools remained singularly insular in their practices and outcomes.

However, the problem can be expressed in another way. Who was served by these endless failures? What was the usefulness of mass institutions that were constantly criticized and continuously reformed? How did they manage to maintain the very delinquency they sought to eliminate? How did they reproduce the endless numbers of drop-outs from one generation to the next, truants and drop-outs they apparently sought to discourage? How did they produce the high rates of academic failure they themselves reported each year? Perhaps it is time to look beneath the apparent attempts at reform. After forcing out large numbers of youth, schools still managed to stigmatize them by depriving them of certification they needed to go on to higher levels of learning or work. The high school diploma became an important entry into the workplace for millions of young men and women. Are not these practices, then, a way of streaming children into a stratified labor market? The schools seemed bent upon educating the immigrant and urban poor for their proper places in some future U.S. workplace. It distributed them at an early age and taught them to accept a life of lower expectations. It was not only that society needed to render urban youth harmless and law-abiding, but also that they wished to prepare them for an acceptance of the conditions of work as they existed. Schooling was just another way of handling differences in opportunity and access to a better life, of providing a competition over time, of giving an "objective" accounting of student achievement, of excluding the unworthy and incompetent, of neutralizing feelings of envy, jealousy, anger, and anxiety among those who would be assigned to the lower stations in society. Schooling did not simply note the inequalities in deportment and achievement; it documented them, providing a scientific explanation that made them seem more significant and immutable than they really were. If these scientific theories and tests later were shown to be false, it was only because the middle classes no longer controlled the rage and anger of those whose children were pushed out in the previous methods of appraisal.

The forces of school reform had converged their efforts on the problems of governance, cost-effectiveness, and accountability during the nineteenth century. An entire system devoted to stigmatizing pauper boys originally sought to economize and standardize schoolwork while supporting the infamous Lancastrian schools. A lack of tolerance between the propertied classes and the growing immigrant and urban poor led to the establishment of these schools and to severe regimentation and punishment practices. The common schools then emerged from the ashes of these charity schools, crowding children into congested schools and tightly controlling their bodily movements and their thoughts. Their social backgrounds were disparaged and their languages and cultures demeaned. At the end of the nineteenth century and well into the twentieth, the pedagogic practices of rote learning and military discipline still dominated classroom life.

NOTES

1. John Dewey, *Experience and Education* (New York: Macmillan, 1938), pp. 66–67; Sol Cohen, *Progressive and Urban School Reform: The Public Education Association of New York City: 1895–1954* (New York: Teachers College, Columbia University, 1963), chap. 1, 2.

2. John Dewey, *Experience and Education*, pp. 337–41; John Dewey, *The School and Society* (Chicago, Ill.: University of Chicago Press, 1915), pp. 9–11.

3. John Dewey, *Democracy and Education* (New York: Macmillan, 1933), pp. 225–30.

4. Ibid., pp. 214–17; John Dewey, "An Undemocratic Proposal," in *American Education and Vocationalism: A Documentary History, 1870–1970* (New York: Teachers College Press, 1974), pp. 142–48.

5. Dewey, *Democracy and Education*, pp. 244–47; John Dewey, "A Policy of Industrial Education," *New Republic* 1 (December 19, 1914): 12–13.

6. Michael B. Katz, *Class, Bureaucracy and Schools* (New York: Praeger, 1972), pp. 113–25.

7. Charles J. Karier, *Foundations of Education: Dissenting Views* (New York: John Wiley and Sons, 1974), pp. 44–53; see Raymond Callahan, *Education and the Cult of Efficiency* (Chicago, Ill.: University of Chicago Press, 1962) for a discussion of educational thinking during this period.

8. Karier, *Foundations of Education: Dissenting Views*, pp. 50–52; Anthony Platt, *The Child Savers: The Invention of Delinquency* (Chicago, Ill.: University of Chicago Press, 1969), pp. 97–99; Edward Thorndike, *Educational Psychology, Briefer Course* (New York: Teachers College, Columbia University, 1914), pp. 348–52.

9. Peter De Boer, "A History of the Early Compulsory School Attendance Legislation in Illinois," cited in Ira Katznelson and Margaret Weir, *Schooling for All:*

Class, Race, and the Decline of the Democratic Ideal (New York: Basic Books, 1985), p. 72.

10.   Colin Greer, *The Great School Legend* (New York: Basic Books, 1972), pp. 105–29.

11.   Lawrence Cremin, *Traditions of American Education* (New York: Basic Books, 1977), pp. 124–28; Greer, *The Great School Legend*, p. 109.

12.   Greer, *The Great School Legend*, pp. 116–17; Joseph M. Hawes, *Children in Urban Society: Juvenile Delinquency in Nineteenth Century America* (New York: Oxford University Press, 1971), pp. 171–72, 244–46.

13.   Lawrence Cremin, *The Transformation of the School: Progressivism in American Education: 1867–1957* (New York: Random House, Vintage Books, 1964), pp. 3–8; Dana F. White, "Education in the Turn-of-the-Century City: The Search for Control," *Urban Education* IV (July 1969): 169–72.

6

New Divisions: The Emergence of the High School

From the Report of the Committee of Ten in 1893 and until the end of the century, the nature and pedagogy of the high school remained in dispute. Educators agreed it was to be a training ground for life in the workplace, but there, agreement ceased. Some believed it should be a training for college, others that it should prepare youth for vocational pursuits. In 1890, only 6.7 percent of the population were in secondary schools. Only 10 to 20 percent actually graduated. By the 1920s, a high school education was almost universally required by the states of the Union, and the old curriculum areas of Latin, Greek, and theology had been replaced by a more secular, scientific course of study. Still, two-thirds of those who entered these secondary schools failed to graduate; approximately one-third of them left before completing the second year.[1]

PEOPLE'S COLLEGES

What were the myths driving this sudden expansion of secondary education? Foremost among them was the notion that such schools would be people's colleges, bridging the gap between elementary education and college training. Educators sought to assure the parents of immigrant and urban youth that all the resources of the state would be used to provide their children with equality of opportunity. All classes were welcomed and promised an education that was all things to all people. To immigrants and working-class families, the high school offered industrial and craft training. To merchants and businessmen, it proposed graduates who would have bookkeeping skills. To the college-bound, it offered courses in logic, language, and science. To the wealthy, it proffered visions of an education that stressed the liberal arts. To those who were concerned about the health and welfare of democracy, the high school promised to provide youth with the insights they would need to participate in self-government. Those were some of the selling points of the system that were presented to the U.S. people. However, the real world of the high school itself was quite different. Although it was being sold as a gesture toward greater equality of opportunity and democracy, its own procedures were increasingly authoritarian, its methods of instruction dominated by rote recitations and a military discipline. Its missions were obscured by the demands of the school organization for order and control in very large buildings. Essentially, secondary education was encouraged as a way of counterbalancing the lack of industrial skills and poor attitudes of the immigrant and urban poor. It was seen as a way of safeguarding the U.S. system during the period immediately following World War I when changes in technology, production, and urban life caused great confusion and discontent in all classes of society. The idea was to place urban youth in surroundings where they would be in constant contact with the more advanced ideas associated with modern life — skills in science, technology, and discipline.

Coercion appeared as an integral part of the organizational structure of the urban high school because of the legal demands of the state. Youngsters were to be confined there during their teens and discouraged from entering the labor market in any significant way, but this only followed in the footsteps of the old common schools and the late nineteenth century reforms. Sites were chosen away from surrounding communities, and high schools of immense size were built so that instruction occurred in isolation and seclusion. Yet, the coercion practiced in these new high schools was of a much greater intensity than anything that had been seen in the lower grades and was the most visible sign of the true nature of these state-funded institutions. The power to transform students, to direct them, and to command their obedience allowed such high schools to function as the sole legitimate means of social mobility in U.S. society. Here youth could not disrupt or disobey without facing stern punishments — they were under complete adult domination and control. The language and culture of the school were imposed upon students who had very different backgrounds from those desired by educators. This variance was the single-most reason why so many students failed and why the schools were so good at keeping these youngsters in their place.

SOCIAL FUNCTIONS OF HIGH SCHOOLS

For these reasons, we must look more closely at the functions of these urban high schools. Incarceration of youth, selection of successful from unsuccessful students, socialization of teenagers into an awareness and acceptance of their standing in society, instruction in the skills and understandings of a stratified, industrial United States, and certification of those who successfully completed the high school work — these were the essential social tasks these "people's colleges" had in common with elementary school counterparts. The work of urban high schools was obsessed with the social tasks state governments gave to it. In the new schooling, military and penal forms of punishment and instruction from earlier periods were refined and given a new rationale. Correction still governed within these buildings, but it was rendered more impersonal by bureaucratic standards and a widely held consensus that teachers were overly directive because of their concern for the welfare of students. Yet, these practices made it impossible for youngsters and teachers to handle the emotions of anger, frustration, and humiliation that were often encountered in these massive institutions. The high school punished the student's failure in deportment, dress, and schoolwork as it had always done in the past, but these practices were made more severe by new state laws that insisted that every teenager was to attend high school, even those who did not possess the skills or inclinations to progress or learn. Relations between teachers and students became more custodial and strained. Curriculum became less effective and relevant when it was taught to students who were not prepared to receive or understand it. As a result, the incompetency of many of these urban youth was confirmed yet again in a series of classroom and examination failures. These proved to be a mere prelude to their dropping out of school entirely.

What were the moral justifications educators used to explain away their work in these schools? How did these beliefs affect the way schoolwork was presented to urban youth? Educators believed that schoolwork and industrial labor possessed a disciplinary and constraining power that was essential to the functioning of modern organizations. For that reason, all agencies in the industrial United States were characterized by scheduled times and places where work was to be done. In the high schools, this constraining force was shown by demands of teachers for greater student attentiveness. Students were to exhibit overt signs that they understood their obligation to master the increasingly specialized curriculum of the high school. Through schoolwork, teenagers learned to respect the authority arrangements and social mores of industrial culture. They submitted to the routines and laws that maintained and strengthened the status quo. Therefore, schooling was to be legally required of youth — they must master it together and according to the judgments of the professional staff.

In the urban high school, schoolwork was separate and apart from the everyday lives of students. It was imposed to facilitate selection and obedience. It was a way of limiting diversity and forcing a submission to order and to responsibility as it was defined by educators. Its chief aim was to provide physical and mental constraints upon the freedom and aspirations of urban youth.

The constant observations and evaluations in continuously changing classroom locations were more uncompromising and less forgiving than they had been in the primary grades. There were written exams that were statewide and that had to be taken by every student in order to graduate from the high school. Any deviation from the accepted responses or behaviors or any disorder, rowdiness, or disruptive acts were punished severely. The teachers invited parents to open-school nights. There, parents learned of their youngsters' achievements and transgressions and promised assistance in helping children to do better in the future. The best face was put on schoolwork, and parents were treated as natural allies in the struggle to educate and socialize the young. These meetings generally dealt with problems of achievement and decorum. It rarely happened that they deteriorated into unpleasant confrontations. The students were polite and attentive when they were allowed to participate. Often, however, these meetings excluded them while focusing upon their behavior and actions inside the school building. Students were still placed in the role of the ignorant and unknowing one and were addressed only later, when teachers and parents had decided upon a common course of action.

These constraints were part of the high school's attempt to control the inner selves of teenagers, to limit their ability to control their bodily movements, and to engage them in work that created feelings of anxiety and inferiority. Education was dominated by a system of rewards and punishments that was supported by a common adult cultural and moral ethos. A science of education was made possible, because under constant observation, students were forced to deny their boredom, anger, and frustrations. They were judged only by their appearances and overt actions. Their intentions and motivations were ignored whenever possible. They were responsible only for that part of themselves that was visible to the teacher. The rest of the human response to constant regimentation was condemned to silence. The observation that searches, that detects, that comes near in order to notate — accepting only the values and procedures of educators — that was the supervision that dominated life in mass urban high schools. The pedagogy of secondary schools, as it developed in these schools, would always be concerned with observation and classification, with social order and control. It would be a one-sided domination by staff that reaffirmed their authority, status, and right to do as they wished in their classrooms.

Students were treated more formally but essentially the same as in primary grades. They had the lowest status in the system, little or no right to bodily autonomy, an no right to be at particular places unless they had the permission of teachers. Everything sought to transform them into compliant, dependent, and machinelike creatures. They were thought of as persons without much energy or imagination and with little sense of how they could work constructively in classrooms. For purposeful behavior, there were rewards; for idlers, there were punishments, as in the charity and common schools of long ago. An old system of control was refined and used while new efforts were made to standardize the movements and thoughts of students. Students were first oriented to the conditions of their new subjugation, then coerced into working at meaningless tasks for many hours each day. Such was the thinking of many during these first decades of the twentieth century.[2] Even the law regarded high school students as minors needing guidance and trusteeship during the school day. Emphasis was placed on the idea that the school was a community of sorts, with its own life, values, and cultural system. This community put the high school students in an environment that was supposedly better suited to their educational needs. In truth, it forced them into an impositional state institution that stripped them of their personal identity and sense of competency. (We will return to this theme in the next chapter.) Here, let us note that the extension of the schooling experience to teenagers was meant to protect them from the abuses of child labor in factories and mills, but, in practice, it forced them to become the object of teacher control and domination — teachers were the ones who knew what was best for students now and in the future.

SOCIAL STRATIFICATION

In the organization of relations between students and teachers, the school community concept played an important role. It separated students on the basis of their social status, educational attainments, and their family's actual standing in the social order. What kind of relationships developed in these impersonal organizations? The student's civil status, as defined by law, was a lower one in which all liberty and freedom were disallowed. The entire educational experience was now enveloped in a moral and familial mythology that sought to justify the coercive actions of educators. The charisma and prestige of the family was used to further validate the surrogate actions of the relentless, driving schoolteacher.

The problem for educators, after the high school became widespread in the 1920s, was to establish a system that would maintain and improve upon the teachings of the lower grades. The benefits of a high school education were offered to all (except for those few who were thought to be too handicapped to cope with its demanding curriculum). This curriculum, of course, was one of the primary means by which teenagers were separated and stratified in the schools. By "curriculum," we refer to those subjects, skills, values, and behaviors that were sanctioned and preferred by educators and boards of education. These provided teachers with a convenient way of selecting out urban youth while socializing them to accept their social and occupational roles in the industrial United States. The high school curriculum was irrelevant to the needs, interest, and experiences of urban youth. Its primary purpose was to legitimate the success of those who came from the better families, those who were destined for college and the better jobs in the workplace. Curriculum made students aware of a body of knowledge outside themselves that had to be mastered if they were to succeed in school. This corpus of knowledge was more meaningful to youngsters coming from more affluent, native-born, middle-class families. They had been tutored since infancy to understand and respond to its language and to the symbolic world speech and language created in their homes and in schools. Curriculum was supposedly a fair competition, educators assured the public. However, the competition was seldom fair. The farther apart the language and content of curriculum was from that of a student's family, the more likely the student was to fail in high school classrooms. The power and influence of those who established and controlled the curriculum was political and economic in nature and helped those who were in positions of power to remain there while deciding in each generation who succeeded and who failed in urban high schools.[3]

Curriculum made children aware of what was and what was not important. It told them what was and what was not worthwhile and interesting. Those who accepted these ideas had the best chance of succeeding in school; those who did not, failed. In this way the educational system maintained and perpetuated itself and the social relations that existed inside the school building and in the workplace. The society and political system accepted the falsehood that schooling was a fair competition that was open to all classes of society.

The relationships between curriculum and the selection processes of high schools led inexorably to the old grade system, to IQ and achievement tests, and to the tracking of the immigrant and urban poor students in neighborhood schools that were structured for failure. Youngsters came to them untutored in the language and educational skills that educators insisted were essential to success in schooling and, later, in the labor market. However, they were unable to provide such skills, even though students spent a great part of their youth in urban schools.[4]

In the race for success and status, children were excluded or included based on the schools they attended, the classes they were placed in, and so on. Those from more affluent families had better linguistic and cultural backgrounds for doing schoolwork. They had better diets, neighborhood schools, and a curriculum in which they had been programmed to succeed. Consequently, symbolic violence was done to the self-images of urban youth in the disguise of fair and open competition. Youngsters were assured that they were disabled and incompetent persons by well-meaning but misinformed teachers and guidance counselors.[5]

The fact that the curriculum was based on speech and language as well as certain types of abstract thinking meant that it could be used as in instrument for selecting out children from immigrant and urban poor families. The curriculum in high schools reflected the experiences, ideas, and language of the educated middle classes. Its abstractions and perspectives were from the experiences common to middle-class individuals. Those who entered with these ideas and linguistic heritages usually did well.[6] Educational curriculums perpetuated inequalities even as the public accepted their propaganda that schooling's practices were democratic and fair, but the public was engaging in a bit of wishful thinking. The curriculum that was outside the mind and body of the learner lent itself to the recitation method, thereby permitting legislators to speak of cost-conscious, efficient education. It encouraged rote learning and passiveness and met the requirements of bureaucratic organizations and the labor market while ignoring those of the individual. Finally, it allowed educators to measure students against one another and to show objective proof of a particular pupil's inadequacies.

In summary, the high schools were instruments of social constraint, in much the same way as their primary counterparts, because they continued to track youth as the lower grades had done; they devised districts that were segregated along racial and class lines; they used curriculum and language that discriminated against the urban poor; they provided urban youth with educational experiences that were predicated upon their presumed occupational status, thus, strengthening the status quo and the youngster's place in the workplace; they assaulted the self of children by forcing them to play the ignorant, incompetent person in state schools; and they created a mythology of fair competition under objective conditions that forced youth to experience their constraint and failures as personal ones.

The high school was an agency of the state, a place of inculcation, of ethical transformation accomplished for the benefits of a diverse society seeking homgeneity. Everything that was foreign was sacrificed to the needs of industrial culture, machine society, and bureaucratic efficiency. The traces of personal identities were erased and replaced by institutional roles and bureaucratic discipline. In the first three decades of the twentieth century, the high schools were asked to bridge the gap between youth of all classes in society. They were ordered to open up their doors to those who had ignored or been excluded from secondary education in the past. The values of work and cooperative enterprise, so important in industry and commerce, now governed the techniques and procedures in these schools, and they were much more effective than they had been in the primary grades. They were able to control the behavior and movements of students during a critical moment in their development. The disorder and confusion of the teenagers seemed to be interested in nothing other than frivolity and idleness. They tried to avoid the routines and schoolwork of the high school whenever possible, but with diminishing effectiveness.

The new secondary schools sought to reduce the differences in appearance and behavior among youngsters. They sought to eliminate all that was spontaneous, irregular, unanticipated, or alien. The task of homogenizing an immigrant and impoverished student population was rigorously pursued into the second and third generation.

However, all this social rejection and regimentation of youth had unintended effects. Indifference and drop-out rates remained unacceptably high into the 1990s! The high school was, in all of its various forms, an agency of moral suasion. It was the state's agency for transforming and denouncing inappropriate behaviors or work patterns. Its task was to impose an arbitrary curriculum and language upon students, forcing them to accept it in place of what they had been taught by their families and friends. The high school was to be a continual reminder to youth of their disadvantaged condition. It acted by constant use of disciplinary procedures that fixed the students' minds on an awareness of their standing in the school and in society. Schools made children aware of their racial, ethnic, and sexual identities and their status in U.S. society. The tracking of youngsters was easily accomplished in high schools. To effect stratification, high schools were also given districts that were already segregated along racial and socioeconomic lines. The better high schools served middle-class teenagers, while the lesser ones served students from the immigrant and urban poor. To refine the system of tracking further, students were placed in classes according to their language and conceptual understandings. These practices assured an ethical basis for the ranking of urban youth in the secondary schools, much as it had done in the nineteenth century primary schools.[7]

DISCIPLINE IN HIGH SCHOOLS

In the first three decades of the twentieth century, poverty, crime and vice were again rampant in urban centers. Youth were arrested and confined in penal institutions in large numbers. High schools were asked to stem the tide of these antisocial forces once again. They were to educate urban youth for more useful and compliant pursuits. They were to be the agencies where the state could train loyal and obedient Americans. Three important disciplinary routines were used to carry through these mandates, once youth were actually attending mass high schools.

No Talking Inside the Building or Classroom

Discipline here had an antisocial bias. The classroom, the prohibitions against moving or talking without permission, the sarcasm of teachers, the public humiliation of youngsters were to urban youth the very core and substance of secondary education. However, these prohibitions had an isolating effect on students and teachers. Both were forced to work much of the time in silence and unison on a curriculum that was uninteresting and irrelevant to both. It was the urban and immigrant youth who were humiliated the most. The constraint of bodily movements reduced the students to the status of infant. The one-way dialogue of constantly talking teachers robbed them of their powers of speech and reason and insulted their intelligence and person. The general response of many of the students was an increasing indifference and inattention to the schoolwork. Their inability to develop relationships with others reduced them to an infantile condition that aroused feelings of frustration, humiliation, and shame. They were regularly disciplined for the smallest of offenses and came to see these punishments as a reasonable response to their youthful transgressions. Thereafter, they would be more forthcoming and punctual, more willing to obey the rules and regulations of the high school without question.

Education in these high schools had a paradoxical effect. The overcrowded classrooms, the rigid schedules, the uniform methods, the constant demand for compliance and obedience, the coerciveness of impositional teachers were, to the students, the real environment within which learning experiences took place. However, the demands for order and obedience, the indifference and silence that was preferred by educators confined students and deprived them of their liberty and curiosity. They were forced to listen to the teacher throughout the day in silent and attentive deference, acknowledging his or her authority by occasional responses to questions or by asking questions. It was the self of children that was assaulted by these practices. The constraint of disciplinary methods in mass high schools caused youngsters to experience solitude among crowds of friends and fellow students. The demands of school routines made it almost impossible not to get into trouble. The most widespread responses and needs of youth were ignored, causing them to respond to their education with indifference, confusion, or passive resignation. As late as 1983, the Center for Education Statistics in Washington was reporting that 32 percent of U.S. students dropped out of school before high school graduation. The students were taught to accept the idea that their failure was a consequence of their lack of purposefulness and will. Teachers were not the ones who were blocking their progress through the grade system: they were not the agents of the students' humiliation and shame. The guilt was the students' alone.

Discipline By Imitation

At the high school, urban youth were observed and were aware of the questioning eyes of teachers. They found it best to conform to the behaviors of older students and to imitate them as best they could. In that way, newcomers tended to become less noticeable, less out of step with others. These were important consequences of an educational experience that stressed socialization and discipline. Imitation and uniformity were encouraged by school authorities. Youth were made to mimic their elders, to come to see the high school through the eyes of others who had come before them.

Constant Evaluation

By the confrontation of youth with their incompetencies, with their failures in schoolwork, examinations, or deportment, teachers finally made students realize that they were as their teachers portrayed them. Any teacher anywhere in the school had the right and duty to observe, judge, or stop any student. These rights were based on the status of teachers in the school community. All of a student's infractions, misdemeanors, and failures were mentioned constantly, helping youngsters to understand, at last, their unworthy and incompetent condition. The discipline of schooling, in all its righteousness, became the mechanism that helped youth to accept their limited opportunities in the schooling community.

In addition to the no-talking rule, to the discipline by imitation, to constant evaluations and punishments, a fourth structure of discipline must be mentioned. This was the glorification of the high school teacher as a specialist and professional instructor of youth. This was doubtless an important idea, because it carried with it the notion of teaching as a calling, a service provided by an occupational group that deserved to be accorded the label of "professional." An old relationship was, thus, affirmed in the secondary schools. Teachers were seen as individuals who cared enough about youngsters to teach them, to correct them, and to provide a realistic evaluation of their work and future potentialities. With this affirmation of teaching as a social service, professional occupation, the ethotic basis for schooling was strengthened and solidified in the minds of the public.

The requirements for entrance into high school were in harmony with accepted ideas in education and the business society. From earliest times, the successful completion of elementary training was needed before a youth could be accepted in secondary schools of any kind. Once in the high school itself, the teacher took a dominant place in the classroom, echoing earlier experience in primary education. All chairs and eyes were placed so they could focus upon the teacher's presence.

However, and this is important, the teacher's right to command was not made by virtue of superior intellect alone but by the commonly held values and assumptions of Americans. It was as a teacher of information and decorum that the staff person had authority. It was as a legal-rational authority that the teacher assumed the duties and prerogatives of a substitute parent and disciplinarian. If schooling was needed in the industrial United States, it was as a moral and ethical force against the vices and inroads of urbanization. A man who was properly obedient, who was of good moral character, who had had a long and successful experience with schoolwork would do well in the factories and offices of industrial society. The high schools were only a small part of the larger social and moral order that must be accepted by youngsters before they assumed their places in the labor market. Parents, churches, the media, the state, and other agencies of the social system must do their part in preparing youngsters with proper attitudes and values.

This adoption of disciplinary methods from other organizations in society was something that was happening everywhere as bureaucracy took control of the institutions of modern society.

1. At first, the high schools were expected to minister only to the college bound and upper middle class, to exclude or discourage those who were unable to afford the luxury of doing without their children's labor, to avoid the debasing of secondary education by making it too readily available to the broad masses of U.S. youth. Now, however, they were asked to recruit, to contain, to teach urban youth of every background and persuasion in order to increase their usefulness to industry and commerce, in order to fulfill the U.S. dream of equal opportunity for all. Discipline was no longer merely a way of preventing disorder and truancy in schools. It had become a series of procedures to enable the congested high school to sustain itself, not as a mere aggregation but as a cultural force that derived from uniformity and routines increased power and authority of educators. Discipline heightened the skills of students, coordinating their efforts and assuring their orderliness. It increased their ability to do schoolwork in the higher grades while broadening the scope and authority of teachers. The discipline of the high school mirrored that of the workshop. It became a force for insuring respect for the authority of schoolteachers, of preventing disruptions in the work, and so on. It increased the efficiency, aptitudes, and productivity of students, and it developed a moral control over the behavior of teenagers. When, in the late nineteenth century, the high schools were founded to replace the old academies, the justification

given was rooted in the changing needs of an increasingly urban, industrialized society. Those who were able to raise their children correctly hoped to prepare them for their obligations in the world of work. Given the changing nature of work and the advantages of a secondary education, they would be better able to occupy places in the universities or managerial positions in the labor market. Now, at the start of the twentieth century, the goals of secondary schools were laid down by prestigious committees, one led by Charles W. Elliott of Harvard. Among other things, the goals of high schools were to prepare urban youth for their futures in the world of work, to give them a deep sense of commitment to work and punctuality, and to train them in a set of competencies that would allow them to calculate and communicate effectively. The goal of secondary schools was a familiar one, of course: train purposeful, useful workers and citizens for the nation, hence, their emergence from a marginal position in industrial society to one of prominence. Rather quickly they were separated from the elementary schoolhouses where they had often resided and placed in more imposing mass structures. From this also followed their role as the inculcators of the language and culture of the United States. High schools became widespread in response to some of the deep-seated needs of the mass industrial United States. Factory production needed workers who could supervise and work on assembly lines, communication industries needed workers who could transmit information over long distances, and the military needed more literate soldiers to man the ever more destructive weapons of war. This last was an important reason that organizations throughout this period increased their emphasis on discipline and regimentation in schools and the workplace.

2. The disciplinary mechanisms of schools was mirrored in those of the corporate United States and in its military and penal institutions. These methods of control seemed to become detached from the religious schools, the armies, and the penal institutions of the past and to lodge themselves as important tendencies in all mass organizations that were forced to deal with huge numbers of people in small spatial areas. Often these disciplinary routines used external surveillance as their primary means of social control. So it was that high schools were provided with counselors who could advise students and parents about the best way to proceed through the maze of choices that now confronted them. The high schools used the information they garnered in observations to educate and direct the behaviors of both parents and students. The poor work or conduct of students or their truancy was a reason for speaking to parents and questioning them about their family practices and

discipline methods. Did they know of these breakdowns in conduct? Did they know that their son or daughter was disrespectful to teachers? Were they doing anything to help their youngsters to improve their work or conduct in school? Were they committed to the moral education of their children and to rooting out evidences of delinquency or vice? Did their youngsters have a place to study? Were they working in the late afternoons or evening? The end of these parental visits was often the same: parents assured teachers that they would discipline and control their youngsters and keep in touch with the school. So, the high school was increasingly accepted as the sole training place for the urban youth of U.S. society. After the expansion of the high schools in the first three decades of the twentieth century, there were several efforts made to modernize the curriculum and to formalize objectives. Vocational courses were now included, and Latin and Greek were quietly removed from the curriculum.

Let us return for a moment to the disciplinary observations in the classrooms of these high schools. Elementary schools had long used these methods to coerce and control their unruly students. Military discipline had played an important role in controlling urban youth during these first years of schooling. From the Committee of Ten onward, high schools assumed the burden of educating the teenagers of the United States. Their goals were moral (moralization and Christianity), economic (encouraging youth to work with resolve), and political (struggling to contain the poverty and urban crime that now threatened to engulf the nation's cities). Districts were formed according to socioeconomic levels of the families who lived within them. They were divided so that children were tracked into better or poorer high schools, much as they had been in the lower grades. The tracking then was refined by organizing classes that reflected the abilities and deportment of their students.

3. Police powers were now given over to teaches and administrators. In high school, it was administration who carried through the ultimate forms of discipline and control. In the classrooms, the role of disciplinarian was in the hands of the state-certified teacher. The teacher was asked to order and control the members of the class and did this with his/her personality and the disciplinary system of the school.

The introduction of disciplinary deans was an expression of the increasing specialization of staff that followed the triumph of bureaucracy in the industrial United States. The teaching staff wanted an educator who was directly concerned with disciplinary matters, one who was available during the day to receive malcontents and disruptive students who were upsetting class routines. In establishing this position over school discipline — the containment of unruly students, buildingwide surveillance of student movements and decorum, supervision of large areas and congregations of youngsters — the deans refined disciplinary practices so that they were more technical and efficient. All the significant problems in the high school were ultimately handled by these new experts in order and control.

Of course, the kind of powers these deans exercised was still constrained by administrative procedures. They were offices that had to be in harmony with the principal and his assistants while at the same time concerning themselves with the details of student-teacher disputes. The dean must do something about every student who was sent to the dean's office. The dean was not the final arbiter of a student's fate and punishment, except when the infractions were minor and the punishments routine. The deans were concerned with those things that were brought to their attention, those things about which the principal did not want to concern himself/herself. With the high school deans, one is in the world of police power as it was finally formalized in the urban secondary schools.

These deans were also given power to scrutinize students in the yards, lunchrooms, and hallways in order to make judgments about recalcitrant and disruptive youngsters. They transformed the high school experience into an exercise in perception and surveillance. Malfunctioning was seen as a deviation from the normal, expected ways of doing things. The results of these police procedures were followed up in interviews and reports. Throughout the 1930s and into the modern era, an enormous amount of paper reports covered the actions and behaviors of youngsters as they worked and studied in overcrowded urban high schools. What was written in these reports was considered as valid evidence by suspension boards when they examined the behavior and attitudes of youngsters who were being considered for expulsion or worse.

Although the deans were under the nominal control of administrators, they sometimes functioned in an independent manner. They were in lower middle management positions. They had to respond to the demands of teachers immediately and to request suspension hearings when the evidence warranted. At the same time, they had to train teachers to perform their own disciplinary acts on students as a first line of controlling the numbers that came to their offices. The deans punished by confinement. A series of lesser misdemeanors was met with detentions; these included classroom disorder or disrespect, disruption, disobedience, unruly conduct, and other behaviors that detracted from the purposeful activities of the classroom. In short, the twentieth century high school refined the policing procedures of the past and appointed specialists to pursue student order and control inside the building.

Discipline, as we have noted earlier, is a form of power that comprises an entire complement of methods, procedures, levels of application, and so on. It is a technology concerned with coercion and the control of the students' bodily movements, and it may be exercised by specialized staff or by teachers and parents. It is a way of strengthening the power and authority of educators and adults during these difficult teenage years.

Discipline was the art of surveillance. Educators searched for the uniform responses that were expected of students, noting those who were apparently not paying attention or burying their heads in classwork. Behind these demands for such behaviors was the need to train workers in industrial society. The performance of disciplinary structures reinforced the power of those who had been legally sanctioned to reproduce the relationships that existed in schools and society.

The formation of an industrial society obsessed with punctuality, order, and predictable behavior is an outgrowth of historical forces in the economic and scientific fields and goes back to the Industrial Revolution. In schools, and in other bureaucratic, corporate organizations, the methods of discipline were used to insure the social status system of U.S. society. This was (and is) a phenomenon observed in every society known to man: every social order is confronted with the questions of maintaining and reproducing their social relations of production and their cultural heritages. The disciplinary methods of the high school organized themselves around five specific aims: to obtain control over students by referring to commonly held ideological slogans; to decrease resistance of parents and community forces by using separate buildings, classrooms, and detention centers that were partitioned out of view of the surrounding communities they served; to bring the effects of their legal-rational authority to its greatest strength by using them to observe and to correct student actions; to justify this impositional and coercive control of youth by linking it to the outcomes of secondary education and the needs of the business community; and, finally, to increase the usefulness and pliability of students so they could perform more effectively in the mechanistic world of work. These aims of high school discipline coincided with those of primary schools and industrial society. One consequence of the Industrial Revolution and the introduction of high-speed machinery was an enormous rise in the numbers of people living in urban centers. This urban population tended to instability, thereby thwarting the needs of those who sought to fix them in their places so they could be properly utilized by industry. The huge numbers of immigrant and urban poor in U.S. cities forced legal and educational authorities to adopt ever more stringent disciplinary practices throughout the country. By the middle of the twentieth century, armies were counted in the tens of millions and two world wars and a major depression had sapped the energies of the world. These outcomes were associated with the growth of productivity that accompanied industrialization and the problems of economic distribution that characterized capitalism. The development of disciplinary systems throughout society was no doubt linked to these unstable conditions and the rise of bureaucratic organizational practices. Power was built into the structures of political and educational institutions so that they vastly increased productivity and the manageability of legions of workers. This enormous increase in productivity was seen in every organization that survived the transition from agrarianism to industrialism: hospitals developed greater skills and efficiency in delivering health services, schools in knowledge and skills, factories in turning out incredible numbers of manufactured articles, and military forces in the delivery of incredible levels of destructive force.

Societal discipline had to reduce diversity in U.S. society in order to increase efficiency and uniformity. That was why it attempted to control the movements of people within working and school organizations during the normal workday. That was why authorities sought to regulate the habits and attitudes of workers and citizens. What was needed were individuals who could function in predictable ways, thereby allowing industry and commerce to calculate profits, production units, and distribution routes more precisely. Discipline had to neutralize the effects of those who sought to overturn the existing power relations: agitations and organized labor must be stifled, revolts crushed, spontaneous movements discouraged. Anything that tended to bring the immigrant and urban poor into some form of organized resistance to their fate must be destroyed. So, partition was a natural and widely used method in all forms of bureaucratic organization. Within such structures, the timetables, schedules, in-service training, drills, rules, regulations, and surveillance methods were used by management to increase productivity, to make students and workers as good as their machines.

In summary, the high school had the power to correct, to transform, to constantly observe, and to judge students. Teachers also had this power to decide, as well as the authority to decide appropriate penalties for infractions.

This was an important moment in the history of modern life. The high school was situated away from the community it served, making it difficult for outsiders to have any voice in day to day practices. Seen from a historical perspective, these methods of surveillance and control had been used by different organizations for centuries. However, what was new in the high school and other corporate structures was their increase power as knowledge and population exploded across the world. As a result of urbanism and industrialization, the forms of discipline became more objective in their appearances, more refined, and more difficult to ignore. The high school, the hospital, the army, the business corporation became more purposeful, using mechanisms of subjugation that were more difficult to dispute. The ethos that justified such methods was that of mechanical efficiency and the enormous leaps in scientific knowledge and wealth that were produced in each generation.

What was now formalized in the high schools was endless and obsessive discipline. Continuous observations and inquiries into the students' behaviors and academic attainments made school into an onerous and unpleasant experience for many. These constant investigations linked a student's past with the present. A series of evaluations were placed in cumulative files and followed children throughout their schooling experiences. It seemed to absorb more and more information and examination results, allowing educators to place students in their proper tracks in a seemingly objective manner. The public evaluation of immigrant and urban youth in partitioned buildings was the natural consequence of these methods of police surveillance and discipline. The method of placing youth under unchanging scrutiny and supervision was a natural extension of a disciplinary system that was based on rewards and punishment. Is it any wonder, then, that the high school became a major part of the socialization process in modern society? The uniform, impersonal classrooms became widely accepted by generations of students and parents. Their geometric constructions and uniform detail seemed to mirror life in the larger society. Their coerciveness prepared youth for the rigors of life in the world of work, teaching them their preferred behaviors of a mechanistic social order. Is it any wonder that such schools resembled prisons, detention centers, factories, hospitals, and other agencies of state regimentation and control?

NOTES

1. David Tyack, *Turning Points in American Educational History* (Waltham, Mass.: Blaisdell Publishing, 1967), pp. 355–57; Ira Katznelson and Margaret Weir, *Schooling for All: Class, Race, and the Decline of the Democratic Ideal* (New York: Basic Books, 1985), pp. 55–56, 169–70.

2. Raymond E. Callahan, *An Introduction to Education in American Society* (New York: Alfred A. Knopf, 1960), pp. 203–7; Lawrence Cremin, *Traditions of American Education* (New York: Basic Books, 1977), pp. 127–29.

3. Paul W. Jackson, "The Student's World," in *The Experience of Schooling*, ed. Martin L. Silberman (New York: Holt, Rhinehart & Winston, 1971); Stanley W. Rothstein, *Identity and Ideology: Sociocultural Theories of Schooling* (Westport, Conn.: Greenwood Press, 1991), pp. 11–14.

4. Nathan L. Friedman, "Cultural Deprivation: A Commentary on the Sociology of Knowledge," *The Journal of Educational Thought* 22 (1976): 2–3; Stanley W. Rothstein, *The Voice of the Other: Language as Illusion in the Formation of the Self* (Westport, Conn.: Praeger Publishers, 1993), pp. 20–23, 47–56.

5. Peter Berger and Theodore Luckman, *The Social Construction of Reality* (New York: Penguin Edition, 1971), pp. 23–29; Willard Waller, *The Sociology of Teaching* (New York: Russell & Russell, 1932).

6. Howard S. Becker, "Social Class Variations in the Teacher-Pupil Relationship," *Journal of Educational Sociology* 25 (1962): 451–65; Pierre Bourdieu, *The Inheritors: French Students and Their Relation to Culture* (Chicago, Ill.: University of Chicago Press, 1979), pp. 3–9; Pierre Bourdieu and Jean-Claude Passeron, *Reproduction in Education, Society and Culture* (Beverly Hills, Calif.: Sage Publications, 1977).

7. Richard Rothstein, "How Tracking Works," in *Demystifying Schools*, ed. Miriam Wasserman (New York: Praeger Publishers, 1974), pp. 61–73.

7

Agents of the State: Ambivalence in the Teacher's Position

The language of learning did not exist in these schools for the poor, where indoctrination and rectification were fundamental objectives.[1] Nevertheless, instructional processes and curriculums did develop. Successive curriculums were devised for students who could not speak the language and came from faraway, unfamiliar civilizations. Their goal was not so much to educate as to demean, by holding the student's speech and culture up to that of the school itself. The student's attendance was proof of his or her need for instruction: whence those incessant practice drills that numbed the intellect and taught youth to comply at all costs.

There was in the instructional act, even in its most benevolent forms, an element of subjection and resignation. If, in urban schools, the students were exposed to continual surveillance, it was because they could not be trusted to control themselves when they were unwatched: if schoolwork often resulted in confused looks and stares, it was because the minds of students were too unformed, too given to indolence, or too drawn to the baser pleasures; in any event, they lacked the knowledge and understandings they would develop after years of urban education.[2] Beneath the arbitrariness of pedagogic work that seemed to demand continuous tasks of senseless work, there was the command for compliance and surrender to authority; the pupil's indolence and sluggishness were only passive instances of resistance to a process that sought to change the student's personality and self-esteem. What was desired, then, was an educational process that would teach the student the virtues of obedient labor and instill a willingness to persist in meaningless work long after reason would have told him/her to cease. More than the image of subordination and submission was desired, however. The youths must learn to accept the social relations that developed between them and their teachers during their educational experiences together.[3] A spirit must be founded within the children's nature that allowed them to accept, without question, the authority figures that existed in schools and in the workplace.

The ideal educational process involved the transmission of an arbitrary culture and language that masked the social and economic powers supporting such inculcation. To reproduce a stratified economic and social system, urban schooling attempted to represent the classroom and social world, misrecognizing the social relations of production that developed during the educational process. Through language, an attempt was made to describe and understand the social world, without ever dealing with the distortions that developed in this movement from social reality to linguistic categories.[4] Because language was the essence of the urban schooling experience, Louis Althusser and other labeled schools and Ideological State Apparatuses, for example, institutions that used ideological understandings and effects to represent themselves and the social system within which they lived and worked. Amid these ideological and linguistic constructs, the students were formed into socialized individuals who saw the world through ideological sunglasses; political ideals were seen as on-going realities that required little thought or introspection. The teachings in state classrooms were accepted as valid knowledge by students who were being prepared to take their place in an employee society. Teachers presented materials in realistic and empirical ways. Generating in youth an acceptance for what they had been taught by their parents and previous instructors. Finally, to assure students' inculcation, teachers tested and retested them on a variety of skills and factual materials that were learned by methods suggestive of teaching procedures a century earlier.

When students had shown that they accepted urban schools and educators as the transmitters of valid knowledge, a final consequence of urban educational production became apparent: students were seen as having internalized the social relations of educational production as ahistorical, unchangeable givens that must be accommodated but never questioned. This final consequence of inculcation consolidated within the youth the essential elements connecting them to legitimate, natural structures in industrial society.

However, there was no better way of defining the institutional identities of teachers and students than by the use of linguistic categories that were internally logical and superimposed on an essentially external and illogical social enterprise. Language divided and separated, in its speech and usage, all the variant classes that developed in the social relations of economic production. Nothing defined an individual better, nothing could better separate men from their betters; it was a complete system that had its own history and reason for being. How could teachers discover and identify children and scholastic accomplishments without attending to their speech and ability to manipulate and use signification codes? It was when the child spoke that the teacher was able to discern who he/she was and who his/her parents were in the scheme of things. The old example cited in George Bernard Shaw's *Pygmalion* comes readily to mind, in that a common flower girl was transformed into a cultured woman of rank when her ability to speak was radically altered by a speech professor. The power of correct usage, the assurance of proper diction — all these combined to confer upon the well-spoken individual a sense of power and control. However, the language of the poorer classes evoked a different response, condemning them to positions and social standings that were inferior and undesirable.

The structure and meaning of language in classrooms could never be discovered through empirical research alone. Rather, the search had to be for what was beneath the surface of such communications. What was happening to teachers and students as they communicated with one another in classrooms?

Using a command voice, chastising children in front of their peers, separating students according to their deportment and attainments, violence, humiliation of the spirit — instruction in mass schools elicited an endless series of debasements, each of which had a part in preparing youth for the workplaces that awaited them in the adult world.

The ideal training was an institutional one that disseminated the ideas and intentions of forces that were unseen and outside the classroom walls. It consisted of grammatical laws teachers used without consciousness. In classes where immigrants or urban poor predominated, there was a particular language of devaluation that was spoken by teachers without conscious recognition or intent. Attempts to study these linguistic structures were usually ahistorical in nature, with certain communication processes being seen as invariant and ever-present givens in all educational enterprises. Yet, language could not be successfully isolated from the social and economic system within which it flourished, nor could its historical effects be ignored. An unmasking of the communications and curriculum of urban schools necessarily involved an unmasking of the symbolic control and violence inherent in pedagogic actions.[5]

Such unmaskings could be done only if pedagogic actions were studied as ideological communications, helping teachers and students to see the true nature of their work together. The production of educational knowledge had, as its historical and present-day function, the reaffirmation of class divisions by the dissemination of ideology. This, in turn, taught the immigrant and poorer classes to accept their inferior conditions, preparing them to accept the successes of others as deserved in the fair competition of universal schooling.

THE TEACHER'S DILEMMA

The preferred methods of pedagogic communication were those that forestalled disobedience and encouraged subordination. We know that the effective teacher was obliged to use the approved methods and curriculum and had be linguistically correct even when the children could not understand his/her words. We know that students suffered trauma when they gave up their personal individuality and assumed institutional identities. Were not the teacher's constant evaluations of students the same as those that workers experienced in the workplace? Then nothing would be more reasonable than that such practices suffuse the urban schooling experiences of children, the replacement workers of the future.[6] From this came the curriculums that attacked the culture and language of the immigrant and lower classes, seeking either to shame or make students aware of the shortcomings of their heritages, linguistic portrayals that underlined the social and economic differences that segregated in the name of equity and the social norms of order and safety.

To the language of devaluation belong all the disciplinary actions that sought to create the student persona, controlling bodily movements during every moment of the school day. To the structures of the synthesized workplace belonged all the disciplinary aspects of worker subordination and the internalization of the language of legitimate authority. Thus, researchers explained the meaningless work of the classroom as a constant; in schooling, the animal spirits of children were beaten back through a constant application of words and punishments; the child was deprived of needs and desires and submitted to the demands of the student role under penalty of excommunication or failure.

Classroom discipline had the added effect of regimenting students' thoughts and behaviors; they were bombarded with a cascade of words that constructed the social reality of the classroom experiences so that the practice of the past might be strengthened in the present. However, controlling the bodily movements and thoughts of the children produced a stultifying effect. It forced children to regress into the behaviors of an earlier, less developed period of their lives; the impositional behaviors of teachers forced students to respond to the all-powerful and demanding adult, to adopt transferences that they had used in past circumstances.[7] By the end of the primary grades, these practices had apparently triumphed, although the repressions of students assured an adversarial relationship between students and teachers.

The principal task of teachers was to inculcate these values and ideologies of the state, giving rise to the schooled individual. To accomplish this, the chief methodology was a constant correction. Correction had all the immediate virtues of a constant discipline; it achieved its aims by wearing away resistances, it worked its will on everything that was idle, unfriendly, uncooperative, and unyielding in the child's personality. Constant and demanding, it was useful for establishing the order and control that was essential to the learning situation in mass institutions; it established the status system by a series of traditional practices — because it was the right of teachers and adults to order about and control youngsters in every walk of life; there was in corrective discipline coercion without concern, a purifying and socializing power that needed little justification; corrective discipline reduced negative student responses to adult authority: those who experienced it felt that it was legitimate for teachers and adults to guide students and children, fulfilling responsibilities that had their origin in the prehistory of the human species. Corrective discipline was demanding but also necessary if youth were to see things from the perspective of parents and teachers; it was effective in pointing the way for those children whose family lives were disrupted and depressed; several years of elementary school usually eliminated complaints and caused students to assume a compliant and respectful demeanor toward their mentors. For those who did not conform, corrective discipline was associated with unpleasant consequences; however, if students did internalize the discipline of urban schools, their acceptance of the social relations of the larger society were assured.

Quite naturally, rewards and punishments enjoyed a central place in these disciplinary practices, as they had done throughout the nineteenth and early twentieth centuries. Some few believed that the punishment-reward system caused students to strive more energetically, that it helped teachers to identify disruptive and failing students at an early age. More often, however, it was merely the preferred, traditional method of doing things as they had always been done in public schools. Of course, there were difficult children whose behavioral infractions were so serious that they had to be separated from the main body of students. Special punitive schools were often recommended once the normal processes of appeal had been exhausted. Willard Waller was the first to notice the dilemma facing teachers who wanted to "help children" but were forced to teach the standardized and boring curriculum materials and linguistic practices approved by the state. Later research confirmed his findings and showed that such pedagogic practices forced students to accept institutional definitions of themselves, their families, and their prospects in schools and the labor market. Insofar as teachers engaged in learning experiences that were irrelevant to the life experiences of students, their lessons met with passive acceptance or overt resistance from youngsters.

The practice of irrelevant pedagogic actions reached backward to the very beginnings of our educational systems. The rule of absolute silence in classrooms alone bears witness to the functionality and durability of these methods. Such disciplinary controls seemingly were present during the first moments in educational history, when people banded together to reproduce the relationships and conditions of their material existence. In the Middle Ages, the demand for student silence was severe and supported by religious traditions. Lancaster, in the early nineteenth century, was merely copying classroom methods from others in England and elsewhere. According to educators of this period, such practices were the result of organizational pressures: an energetic student body had to be managed and controlled inside congested buildings. They had to be prevented from rowdy behavior that could become a danger to themselves and others. The learning situation required that students sit in silence so they could listen and attend to the teacher's commands. Such images of children sitting at attention while teachers talked about what they were to do, how they were to do it, when they were to do it, and so on are familiar to everyone who has attended public schools.

The truth of these images is as important as the pedagogy of the poor. It conveys in the form of remembered pictures and musings the conditions under which teachers and students came together in crowded classrooms.

The worthiness of these disciplinary practices was of major importance, then and now. From earliest times the silent rule and the regimentation of students held their place at the center of school routines and pedagogic practices. In 1932, Waller detailed the problems that existed between teachers and the students they served in public schools. He noted that the core of the clash between them was the teacher's need to force students to learn the state's prescribed curriculum. Already it was understood that pedagogy that was outside the mind and body of the learner could be used only when it was accompanied by penal and military discipline.

The advantages of these impersonal practices were evident, and their continued use testifies to their functionality in mass educational systems. If students from diverse backgrounds are to be assimilated into the U.S. system and prepared for labor in industrial society, the virtues of the business ethos needs to be firmly implanted at an early age. In fact, the preparation of youth for the labor market was a long-term affair that had to be accomplished over the first 16 years of a student's life. Of course, the constant discourses had their desired effect in preparing an obedient and deferential student body for their places in the adult world. Otherwise, would it have been possible for so many immigrants from so many countries to come to the United States and fit into its ever-changing social and economic ethos? Again and again, educators cited assimilation as one of their most important social tasks. It came first in the minds of many educators and politicians who felt besieged by the silent armies of immigrants that came to our shores in every generation.

However, it can be said just as well that the practices of these public schools served the workplace better than they served the needs of representative government and citizenship. It is exactly this idea that Ira Katznelson, Herbert Gintis, Samuel Bowles, and others have emphasized in their studies of U.S. schools.[8] Public schools imitated the authority structures of work in a competitive, industrial system, but the relationships that developed between autocratic teachers and subordinate and powerless students was bound to carry with it the seeds of ambivalence and hidden resentment, which resulted in those legions of dropouts and failures that the schools documented so well in their yearly reports. However, even these failures were functional for a stratified society in which most of the people would be forced to do menial and unskilled labor. The production of these educational failures helped businesses to control the costs of labor everywhere in the social order.

The paradox of preparing future citizens of the republic by subjecting them to an intensive training in autocratic classrooms was lost on only the blindest of observers. Further, so voracious was the student's need for attention, so great the numbers in urban classrooms that teachers were forced to find ways to control these needs lest they overwhelm them and derail the learning situation. Hand raising itself had to be limited, and, of course, talking was forbidden, because it led to idle time and the disruption of learning. Planning classroom activities was seldom done with the students, who were forced to participate in lessons that would determine their success or failure in schools. Such exclusionary methods gave teachers another reason to keep their distance from the students they served: it might become necessary for them to retain in grade or otherwise punish behavioral infractions or poor schoolwork.

It is precisely for these reasons that students and teachers tended to see one another impressionistically. Friendliness was impossible in a climate that depended upon fear and distrust. The teachers' fear was that they would lose control of their classrooms, while that of students was one of academic failure and disgrace. Also, because students are subjected to a severe discipline for many years, they often become cynical and distrustful of teachers, distorting their actions because of their generalized feelings of anxiety. Because traditional classrooms are constructed so that all eyes are on the all-knowing teacher, information usually flows from the teacher to the students in an endless stream. This makes it difficult for teachers to know how students really feel about them and about the job they are doing in their classrooms. Goals are arbitrarily announced or presented through elaborate forms of persuasion and manipulation. These often lead to student apathy and passivity and a preoccupation with extrinsic rewards and punishments. Resistances surface from time to time, of course, but the demands of constant teacher-motivation speeches indicate that many students enter into the learning situation with only a part of their personal identities. Students are dependent upon their teachers, as they were other adults in their preschool period, and this leads to ambivalence toward all authority figures and the teenage rebellions that are so common in modern life.

Excessive use of impositional behaviors had its effects on the personality structures of teachers, too. Their common problems revolved about discipline and control in mass institutions. It was these obsessional concerns with coercion and restraint that provided observers with their most significant insights into the deeper nature of modern educational systems. In classrooms, it is the task of the teacher to find out whether a pupil has or has not learned prescribed materials, whether a student has or has not measured up to his/her potential abilities, and whether a student is or is not morally fit. The teacher must also eliminate those children who do not fit in, who do not have the intelligence and moral qualities to succeed in the classroom. Teacher evaluations, thus, have the property of defining and promoting a student's direction in schools and the workplace. As many have suggested, the schools are primarily a testing center for children, selecting and distributing youngsters using an academic language and an arbitrary standard.

If it is true that schooling is the symbolic control of children and the subjugation of their minds and bodies, it is also true that this form of work deeply influences the personality development of teachers. An impressionistic interpretation of this occupational category has existed for more than a century: they are described as persons with stiff, formal appearances who are reserved and withdrawn when they interact with adults. Their behavior with students is more mercurial, even though they participate in classroom life in an incomplete and impersonal way. This reserved behavior lacks spontaneity. It hides the teacher's feelings behind a mask of autocratic impositional behaviors. The purpose of these poses is to provide the teacher with a commanding, assured persona when facing the students. A second reason is the desire to hide a second-class mind while presiding over the petty concerns of children. Since the turn of the century, teachers have been described as prudish in manner, speech, and dress.

Teachers, in this impressionistic interpretation of their characteristics, were seen as standing in ways that were always anticipatory, for example, as though they were waiting for students to line up or put their clothing away or get their books out, and so on. However, the most important determinant of these stereotypes was the student-teacher role set that was set up in classrooms. There a dominance-submission syndrome forced both students and teachers to adopt, over time, institutional identities and values. Teachers became more aggressive and domineering in their behavior toward students, even when there were no overt threats to the order and authority structures in classrooms. They became drillmasters without amiability or appeal.

Teachers firmly believed that without these authoritarian personas they could not maintain the necessary order and control needed to construct the learning situation. Simple commands were routinized, using command voices that were without emotion and as automated as a machine. Hair-trigger responses and temper tantrums were common as teachers changed their moods in order to maintain their control over students, who seemed always to be straining at the leash. These efforts sapped the energies of teachers, forcing them into unyielding attitudes and behaviors. As each new class sat down, they were subjected to the changing attitudes and commands that assured teachers their dominating position in classrooms. Waller especially believed that these obsessive concerns with coercion and control drove teachers to impose their definitions of schoolwork upon students. Students were forced to obey these impositional commands of teachers and to play out the role of the ignorant person. Those who had been licensed by the state to act as guardians of the U.S. scene were duty-bound to resist all efforts at compromise when their authority or directions were challenged by students. They must know that they are the ones who must maintain the social relations in schools and society by making constant demands upon the thoughts and attentiveness of children. The teacher's work was seen as a mass of overwhelming routines with few opportunities for self-expression or creativity. Teaching was seen as the sheltered profession, the place where unmarriageable women and unsaleable men ended up. It was concerned with the affairs of children and usually adopted as an occupational choice only as a last resort. New teachers never seemed to be capable of teaching during their first weeks in schools. In desperation, they usually fell back on behaviors and habits they had learned in their own schooling experiences a generation earlier.

These impressionistic interpretations have made teachers defensive and unfriendly toward outsiders and critics. Of course, teaching brings out other, more positive traits in some. To many, it is a call for self-sacrifice and a life of service lived away from the competitive occupational world of adults. Some teachers learn to be more patient and fair to students, to use their teaching as an avenue for self-growth and development. These comments are meant to assure the reader that there are many responses to the teaching situation, but these are usually ignored by those who see teachers in stereotypical ways.

Nevertheless, the most important relationship for the teacher is the one with the students. It is in the classroom that the teacher's responses to students shape his/her personality and character. The relationship between teachers and students is shaped by the demands of the state and school district: constant conflict and tension are assured once the teacher begins to force children to attend to the formal curriculum of the school. Every teacher tries to teach students the things they should know, even when they are unprepared or uninterested in such learnings. When students resist, punishment systems are called into play, with unpleasant results for the teacher-student relationship. The teacher tries to control every situation in the classroom with talk, autocratic mannerisms, and stern voice tones. The speech of a teacher is his/her single most important weapon in the struggle for supremacy and the one that most determines his/her effectiveness in the classroom. The voice is the instrument of communication and instruction, alerting children to what is expected of them. Its pitch communicates impersonal authority and command, its volume and intonation dictate immediate and compliant responses in overcrowded classrooms.[9] The teacher tries to present a cool and competent exterior in every situation, using the voice to mask inner feelings of anxiety or fear. Thus, the tone of a teacher's voice alerts students to how serious a teacher is about a particular command, how much discussion will be tolerated, and so on. Students try to read the deeper meanings of their teachers' words, trying to pierce their mechanistic exterior. Effeminate voices are thought to be bad for classroom teachers because they are associated with the adolescent age and cast doubt on their teacher's authority and command. Students seemed to resent this kind of voice in teachers, constantly challenging their power.

Another voice that was unfortunate for teachers trying to maintain order and control in crowded urban classrooms was one that was overly strained and laden with emotion. The unintended messages were often filled with anxieties or excessive evidences of bravado. An affectionate voice was not a remedy for this unfortunate situation, either, because it interfered with the impersonal, institutional authority teachers were supposed to assert in their classrooms. Waller describes other consequences of such unfortunate voice qualities. Students became anxious and confused or openly hostile and belligerent. If the teacher's voice seemed overly emotional, it was almost certain to evoke strong responses from children, the voice that seemed blustery begged for some challenging response from students, and so on. The teacher, by the threatening demeanor he or she assumed, won and lost students as he/she carried out punishments against some of them. Overly affectionate teacher attitudes led some students to believe that the teacher was playing favorites and was being unfair.

However, the agitation of teacher voices strained with tension created a shrill and nervous environment for students to learn in. Unintended messages were sent and received both on a conscious and an unconscious level, and communications between teachers and students were further confused.

The best voice was that of the dry, impersonal, and precise drill sergeant. This was because the teacher's role was that of the constantly talking authority, the supplier of facts, information, and corrections.

Because teachers did not wish to raise questions about their pedagogic or disciplinary methods, their primary communication procedures were that of the discourse. Facts must be presented and repeated again and again to take on added meaning. Teachers must present them in authoritative voices devoid of emotion, confusion, doubt, wonder, argument, or questioning. Commands must be given throughout the school day, ordering students about so they know where they must go, where they must remain, what they must do in classrooms, and so on. Of course, a more human voice would be better for the psychological health and well-being of students and teachers. It would present a message of acceptance and encouragement. However, state-funded schools demand that teachers maintain their distances from students and their parents.

Those whose livelihoods depend upon controlling the movements and thoughts of children must be suspicious even of humor. Many teachers never smile at the children, feeling that their right to decide everything in classrooms must be preserved at all costs. Such teachers lose the personal contact with students and often teach in hostile, defensive environments. Others do try to distance themselves from the odious role of state representative or bureaucrat, using smiles and humor to lessen the conflicts they have with students. Laughter is a dangerous thing for schoolteachers, and many classrooms are characterized by a humorless and intense conflict between them and the children they serve. Ridicule and sarcasm are often used when students do not obey or otherwise act in inappropriate ways.

Conflict is at the center of the teacher-student role set because of the evaluation powers teachers possess. These insist on labeling children as ignorant, incompetent, and unworthy persons as soon as they enter the school and begin playing out the student role. Subordination is possible only when children believe that teachers are working for their common good. Even so, many children withdraw from the classroom situation in order to protect themselves from the abuse heaped upon them by over-zealous teachers. Teachers need what they have always had in these schools for the common people: they need a mechanistic acceptance of their right to decide things inside the school building. Many students respond to this by behaving in passive or overtly hostile ways. Teachers, reacting as they always have, usually punish the overt offenders while ignoring their more disturbed, passive miscreants.

Because silence and limited movement were the core of classroom discipline, those who experienced it were forced into repressive and regressive attitudes and behaviors during their classroom experiences. Teachers seem unaware of these behaviors, which make it so difficult for them to communicate effectively with students. In the students' role, however, it is infantile behaviors that must be remastered and attended to during the school day. By sitting still in their seats, they revert to an earlier age when they were unable to move about by themselves. By keeping silent, they reenact the dependent and helpless realities of their infancy. By succumbing to the power and control of new adults, they often transfer behaviors from earlier situations when they were also powerless and dependent upon the good will of adults. The teacher, in place of the parents, reproduces the moments in a child's development when the child was more uncertain of himself/herself and his/her abilities. A new code of behavior is used to evaluate the students and their schoolwork. As long as they accept their roles and do what they are told, they are admired and rewarded by teachers. No wonder, then, that students often distrust the adults who are supposed to be helping them; no wonder that they begin to doubt teacher assurances of good will.

This structure of schooling by surveillance is one of the most debilitating aspects of modern educational practice. It is reinforced by constant testing and the anxieties such rituals create in the minds of children (and parents). The comparisons with other students deeply trouble and confuse many youngsters, forcing them to look dependently at teachers and their preferred standards of behavior and work. Because these methods are at the core of educational functions in industrial society, teachers often insist that students become ever more standardized in their responses and behaviors. The price for these demands is high: youngsters in classrooms respond to one another with a segment of their personality, that part that seems to accept their dependent and incompetent status in the school. Because teachers do not allow students to express their negative emotions and responses to school life, they are unable to know their students as persons. Developing new routines and ways of doing things becomes impossible, and pedagogic approaches that might focus upon student needs become a rarity.

Used to meet the demands of mass institutions and industrial society, the pedagogy of the poor insists upon the idea that teachers must control the minds and bodies of students. It is their responsibility, as paid state employees and agents of social control, to teach youngsters to fit into the demands of public schooling and, later, industrial society. We see how even in the everyday classroom routines, the means of inculcation and control are encountered as part of a great organizing structure of modern social systems.

Of course, all societies use these reproductive methods. They all try to reproduce the social relations and conditions of their existence. How else can they get people to do the things they must do if their society is to survive? How else can they be made to play out the roles assigned to them by their birth and standing in the social order? In our own time, however, the social consensus that seemed to exist in earlier periods of U.S. history appears to have broken down. Immigrant and urban poor families continue to be with us in ever more alarming numbers, and even the middle class seems to be slipping backward. As in the past, the time and energy teachers use to keep students busy and under constant surveillance and control turns many of the students off to learning and to schooling itself. Because the schoolwork is boring and pedagogically deformed, it soon becomes obvious that the quest for deferential, docile, and passive students is an obsession in U.S. schools. Perhaps these practices are grounded in the needs of the autocratic workplaces of the industrial United States, but they have not served to create citizens who function well in a democratic society.

THE PEDAGOGY OF THE POOR

These notions of pedagogy were fixed, in the late nineteenth and early twentieth centuries, between a definition of instructional levels and an explanatory principle concealed in the very language and ideology of public schooling. Among the symptoms we find all the contradictions and criticisms educators tended to ignore or explain away. Many thought of the failure of millions of urban and immigrant children in mathematics, science, and language arts as the results of personal failings, separate and apart from public schooling itself. Others refused to admit that urban schools were moving farther and farther from their stated goals. In more recent times, social scientists have come to believe that the pedagogy of the poor was (and is) characterized by inculcation and the state's need to reproduce the status quo in classrooms and society. The public schools, these scholars wrote, mindlessly passed on an arbitrary cultural design, and schoolteachers autocratically taught the speech and language of the educated classes. However, sensible people refused to believe that teachers were passing on arbitrary cultural and linguistic beliefs without being fully conscious of it. Patriotic themes prevailed from one reform period to the next, and teachers went on assuming that their impositional, punishment-dominated classrooms were performing an important social service: the transmission of those elements of U.S. culture that were of the highest order. Many educators were unaware of their role in preparing youth for their places in the workplace and seemed uninterested in examining the social power and ideologies that lay beneath their pedagogic practices. Thus, educational systems performed certain economic and social functions in society without the awareness of staff members and clients alike. Both were compelled by the state to reproduce the social relations that existed between people in the schools and in the labor market.

These new criticisms of modern pedagogic practices posed difficult questions for schoolteachers: Did their teaching practices in urban classrooms lead to symbolic violence and control over their students, as many scholars suggested? Positive responses were given by those who studied and analyzed pedagogic action, the central relationship in the schooling experience. It was in such interaction that children were regularly subjected to symbolic violence and control. It was in the act of instruction that an arbitrary language and cultural preference was dictated to students as the one and only correct one. Teachers and students learned to accept these value systems and symbols without question during their own schooling experiences; it was something to which they were exposed at birth, and they seldom questioned it.

The language and culture of children from the immigrant and poorer classes were most flagrantly excluded from this arbitrary cultural system of the schools. The authority teachers displayed in their classrooms was deceptive in itself, because it tended to mask the power of governing groups who imposed their meanings on the public education of the poor. Pedagogic work was symbolic control, because it added its own force to classroom insights and understandings, given them a legitimacy that further hid from view the power relations existing in both urban schools and the society.[10]

From the outset, then, the distinctive nature of pedagogic action remained poorly defined by traditional educators. We know that the teachers' power to determine what was studied in classrooms was very impositional in nature, allowing for the inculcation of arbitrary political, religious, and cultural values. More recently, scholars have come to understand that the arbitrary (academic) language and culture of urban educational systems determines the kind of social and psychological experience they will have in their classrooms.[11]

This provided further insight into the failure of the poor to do well in schools. Success or failure was always associated with the different social and scholastic backgrounds of students. It was a result of the distance between students' home culture and language and that of the urban schools they attended.[12] This variance was (and is) the source of the inequalities in academic achievement of children from different social origins and sexes in the past and in our own times.

The discussion of pedagogic action remained fixed within a technological tradition until the work of European social scientists. These researchers discovered cultural and linguistic competencies, or capital, stratified students. For Pierre Bourdieu, the pedagogic authority and practices of teachers really did do what everyone had always assumed they did. There was an organic need of social systems to reproduce themselves, Bourdieu wrote, echoing the work of Emile Durkheim. Our workplaces and urban schools were given over to an educational production of knowledge that seemed most interested in maintaining and reproducing the linguistic and cultural basis of present-day social structures.

Remembering the history of schooling in the United States, we can appreciate this hidden nature of pedagogic action: it was (and is) the ultimate form of symbolic control in mass society, encompassing children in a world of words from their earliest days. Pedagogic acts began in the families of children when they were taught the language and culture of their people. The distance between these learnings and those of the schools (scholarly mastery of scholarly language) was the best predictor of a student's success or failure in urban school.[13] "Culture" was used by researchers to refer to the product of the internalization of the principles of arbitrary cultures that had no support in science, logic, or rational thought. Public schools demanded a competency in an arbitrary cultural and linguistic knowledge they themselves could not provide for the masses of students from working-class and lower middle-class families. Such competencies and understandings were provided by a child's family and were mastered through a form of linguistic and cultural osmosis rather than in formal classroom lessons. The educational system, therefore, gave an unfair leverage to those who already possessed substantial advantages, valuing highly the culture and language of upper middle and elite classes. They sought to reproduce their beliefs, values, and social relations in schools and society. Thus, educational advantage confirmed and legitimized the positions of those who had inherited cultural and linguistic "capital" from parents, and the status quo became an overwhelming force in the schooling of urban youth.[14]

What was the role of schoolteachers in these processes of symbolic violence and social control? Without thinking about what they were doing, teachers transmitted their versions of the preferred culture and language they had learned to imitate and admire as students when they were in school. Only occasionally did some see the effects their impositional behaviors were having on the self-systems students.

In the normal scheme of things, this emphasis on the beliefs, values, and style of the elite forced everyone to value highly their experience and world views. Knowledge, both social and academic, gave some students an advantage over others, and the problems of social and economic inequality were passed on from one generation to the next. What were the consequences for other groups, such as minorities and women? Researchers found that women, especially, were unequally selected downward, according to their social origin and sex.[15]

The irony was that, from the beginning, the linguistic and cultural learnings in children's families were capable of explaining, in a systematic way, the relations that came to exist between teachers and pupils in urban schools. If educators could choose any one set of variables to explain the stratification realities of urban education, it was the students' acculturation and language proficiency.[16] The influence of language showed itself in the earliest years, when linguistic abilities were used to measure and assess students' competencies and worth in public schools. These never ceased to be felt, identifying and segregating students from one generation to the next in terms of race and socioeconomic class.

That there were other forms of communication in classroom life was not to be doubted. We know from numerous studies that the pedagogic acts of parents and teachers provided, along with richer and poorer vocabularies, a "complex set of categories, so that the capacity to decipher and manipulate complex structures, whether logical or aesthetic, depended partly on the complexity of the language and world views transmitted by the family."[17] However, the cultural boundaries of an individual's life were set by the beliefs, values, and understandings of the world he or she learned in families. Therefore, we may conclude that educational failures and drop-outs increased as one moved toward students in socioeconomic classes most distant from the arbitrary language and cultural practices of the urban schools, for example, from the language and ideology of schooling. These ideas provided socio-cultural perspectives for understanding an individual student's success or failure in public schools. There, for example, success or failure was measured as a relationship between a student's possession of cultural and linguistic capabilities, his or her father's occupation, and the family's level of academic achievement.

However, an understanding of the disparity that existed between the achievement scores of men and women required further analysis. Several studies in Europe and the United States attested to a constant superiority of men over women. These outcomes were traced to a systematic social conditioning in which women were streamed into lower status careers while men were encouraged to study medicine, science, and law. These studies indicated that women, principally through the processes of initial familial and educational learnings, were victimized by their social origin and sex: the educational establishments they attended predetermined their educational fate, much as the fate of minority children was determined by forced incarceration in urban ghetto schools. These first socialization experiences were strengthened by subsequent learnings and career choices that assured female students less opportunity and success than their male counterparts.

Still, Bourdieu noted that the character of selection survivors in higher education was constantly changing as new criteria came to govern elimination processes. This tended to weaken the relationship between social origin and linguistic competence. Nevertheless, the sons of senior executives were on the top of the university system, studying high status disciplines.[18] Social origin, with its initial socialization and learning patterns, could not be considered as a factor capable of explaining every attitude, opinion, and practice in a student's schooling experiences. The constraints of the selection system had to be understood by examining particular urban educational systems at different moments in their history and development.

It should be noted, too, that Bourdieu did describe an array of social characteristics and associations that defined the first experiences and conditions of children from different social classes. He did this in order to better understand the different probabilities that the various educational experiences would have for them and the significance for individuals in different social classes of finding themselves in situations of greater or lesser prestige and status. For children of manual workers, for sons of laborers, it was highly improbable that they would study Latin and Greek in urban schools; it was more probable that they would have to work if they decided to stay in urban school and pursue a career in higher education.

It may be argued from this that educational systems were (and are) devoted to a pedagogy that affects the way children see themselves, their families, and their occupational possibilities, but this leads us back to the idea that social classes in France, England, and the United States require a selection system that has its beginnings in familial and urban educational experiences of children. That there are stronger and weaker classes of people, affecting the ways each live in society, is seldom contested. Urban educational systems are more and more exclusively involved in providing a pedagogy that is received as symbolic control or violence by students from lower-class families, and these pedagogic practices appear to mirror conditions in the world of work, as they did in the past. This accounts for the huge failure rates reported by urban schools each year.

More and more, we are coming to understand how the process of social reproduction strengthens the existing culture and social relations of familial, social, and educational institutions. We assume that previously held ideas of class struggle and conflict have some basis in fact. Our urban schools resemble the factories and bureaucratic work environments, preparing youth for a working experience that emphasizes worker subordination.

Where do these ideas lead us? Where is urban schooling in the process of social reproduction all social systems strive to accomplish? What is the relationship between urban education and the political, economic, and social structures of modern industrial society?

In every effort of the state to educate its young, there has been an effort to perpetuate the culture and arbitrary assumptions of influential groups and classes; it is as a function of inculcation, social communication, and legitimate social selection that relations between the classes have been maintained in each generation. Efforts to school the young are a profoundly conservative endeavor, as Emile Durkheim taught more than a century ago. However, can this justify current pedagogic practices in urban schools, where symbolic violence and control are accompanied by authoritarian organizational structures and where the adoption of the crudest forms of coercion and control persist even as we approach the twenty-first century? What have schoolteachers done by providing rationales for the social inequalities in modern society? How can pedagogic practice escape the debilitating effects of such antidemocratic practices?

PEDAGOGIC AUTHORITY AND WORK

The intolerable irony in our dissatisfaction with current pedagogic work is that we have largely ignored the structural and sociopolitical aspects of such problems.[19] The function of speech and language in the pedagogic act has rarely been studied or understood, and the social relations that exist in modern industrial society have been ignored. If we were to choose one characteristic of education in Western society, it would be the concealment of the power relations that exist in public schools and the larger social system. There are, of course, many ways to legitimate existing culture: What is the nature of authority in a particular society? In whose interests does it perform its work? How is such authority and power legitimized in the eyes of citizens and workers? These issues have been studied by Max Weber and others and can provide a deeper understanding of the social movement from feudalism to capitalism. They point to legitimate culture as a consensual one having its roots in traditional, charismatic, or legal-rational practices. In times of great ferment and change, charismatic leaders and authorities have often come to the fore, receiving validation from their personality or messages.[20] An attempt is then made by those who follow the charismatic leaders to sustain their teachings in organizations; this is done by resorting to traditional forms of domination. In our own period, however, legal-rational authority, based on laws and the bureaucratic organization of Western society, has become ascendant.[21]

We can suppose, then, that modern schooling's authority rests on legal-rational sanctions and the traditions that have grown up around it. These desensitize us to the symbolic violence and control of the pedagogic acts of teachers, assuring a reinforcement of the predominant assumptions of society itself.[22]

Ultimately, schools have no other choice but to reproduce the principles of the arbitrary culture of the state and society.[23] This is because the language and culture of schooling is imposed by groups and classes who are in control, groups considered important enough to have their values and social relations reproduced by the next generation of citizens. Their worthiness is enhanced, in modern society, because they have apparently delegated to a neutral agency (urban schools) the authority to perform this essential task of social reproduction. It is possible, then, to measure academic success in terms of whether schooling does or does not perform its primary function of inculcation, whether it does or does not reproduce the existing culture and social relations of production.[24]

That pedagogic work can be boring is borne out by recent research and the writings of observers throughout U.S. history.[25] If it does not last over many years, however, important sources of pedagogic power and control are lost. Educators and politicians are the ones who have always defined when a youth has had enough schooling. They decide when he or she is competent enough in the arbitrary curriculum and culture of the urban schools, when enough training has occurred so that an educated person has been reproduced. In addition, they use pedagogic discipline as a substitute for social control and physical constraint: they force students to sit and attend by bringing sanctions against those who fail to accept and internalize the culture and arbitrary pedagogic actions of teachers. Pedagogic work is a form of symbolic coercion and constraint, an action that forces students to sit in classrooms long after they have dropped out intellectually and emotionally. The longer the process of enforced schooling, the easier it is to conceal the truth of the arbitrary language and culture that state urban schools impose on students. Every movement of the dominant educational and social forces in society is toward legitimacy, attempting to validate its own values, history, and language while excluding those of the immigrant and urban poor. Those from the poorer classes find themselves excluded from the benefits of schooling because they are subjected to a symbolic experience that questions their self-worth and competency.[26] Compulsory education forces the oppressed classes to recognize and accept the schools' version of knowledge and know-how. Pedagogic work produces a primary culture and approved language that is characteristic of those who control the economic and social power of the nation. They identify and transmit valid knowledge and behavior from one generation to the next. As in pedagogic action, the degree of effective pedagogic work is a function of the distance between the language and culture urban schools have inculcated into their students and the previous language an pedagogic actions of parents. The success of a student depends upon his or her family and preschool years, even though urban schools perpetuate the ideology that all children start schooling on an equal footing. The acquisition of language, skills in solving everyday problems, kinship relationships, logical forms of thinking, and worldly perspectives are mastered during a youngster's formative years, when he or she learns the language, culture, and class position of his or her family. These beliefs, attitudes, values, self-concepts, and perspectives are symbolic in nature and tie one to a particular class in society, predisposing children unequally toward a symbolic mastery of the pedagogic action and work in classrooms.

URBAN EDUCATIONAL SYSTEMS

The question we need to answer about educational systems is an important one that cannot be answered by research alone: Can an educational system survive without reproducing the social relations of educational and economic production? The central function of state schooling is one of inculcation and indoctrination, reproducing the conditions of schoolwork and the workplace.[27] State-supported schools live by the largesse and direction of the political sectors of the nation; they are duty-bound to validate the conditions and values of society and to segregate those who do not live up to their cultural values.

What the pedagogy of the poor excludes is knowledge that might lead to dissatisfaction with the way things are in schools or the labor market; such understandings would make it more difficult to create and maintain the institutional conditions that have existed in the United States for many years. Educational systems cannot be understood by searching their historical and social conditions alone. Emile Durkheim, however, disagreed with this idea.[28] He sought to understand the nature of educational systems by looking backward to the early Christian habitus and Greco-Roman heritage. Looking at the organizational structures and practices schooling adopted as it tried to solve the problems of a particular period, he used history as a study of an evolving life form. More recently, other social and educational theorists have come to believe that only by examining such structures more intensely could they come to see and understand the social forces that gave rise to different historical situations and educational processes. Only then could they examine educational structures and their relationship to ongoing forces in other sectors of society.

Progress made by an educational system, such as paying teachers, organizing and training them systematically, the standardization of educational organizations over a wide area, examinations, civil service status, and so on, was all part of the bureaucratic establishment and institutionalization of pedagogic work. Durkheim identified the medieval university as the first educational system in Europe because it had within its structure evaluation methods that validated the results of inculcation (the diploma). This evaluation component was Durkheim's primary consideration because it united the pedagogic action of inculcation and forced it into a more homogeneous, standardized pattern. Weber might have added that such urban educational systems were also characterized by a cadre of specialized personnel whose training, recruitment, and careers were controlled by the institution and who found, in the educational system, a way of maintaining their calm to a monopoly of legitimate inculcation of the arbitrary habitus or culture of the urban school and society.

Because modern educational systems cannot perform their essential function of inculcation unless they produce and reproduce the structural and relational conditions for their own pedagogic work, a habitus as homogeneous and durable as possible in as many students and teachers as possible is necessary, and its external functions of cultural and social reproduction force it to produce a habitus as close as possible to the arbitrary culture that funded and mandated it.

The need to assure homogeneous and orthodox schoolwork forces educational systems to move toward standardized training for both teachers and their students. Standardized curriculums, pedagogic methods, and tests are used to measure students against one another. The tools of teaching that the educational system uses are not only aids in the performance of pedagogic action but also ways of limiting the goals, perspectives, and content of classroom work. Textbooks, syllabuses, manuals all have the effect of unifying what is taught in different classrooms by different teachers. The need to codify and systematize the pedagogic communication and urban school culture is conditioned by the demands for homogeneity and orthodoxy in increasingly strained, mass societies. All learning in urban educational systems is done within the framework of an essentially apprenticeship system in which the student is socialized out of his/her ignorant condition over a period of many years. This binds the graduates, teachers, and students to the educational system and to the economic and social system.

The institutionalization of modern pedagogic action is characterized by obsessive concern with reproduction.[29] There is an inadequacy of research training and inquiry methods up and down the grade system. There is a programming of the norms of research and the objects of inquiry is that the interests of the status quo are served. Modern educational systems are relatively autonomous institutions, monopolizing the legitimate use of symbolic violence and serving groups or classes whose cultural arbitrariness they reproduce.

NOTES

1.   Pierre Bourdieu and Jean-Claude Passeron, *Reproduction in Education, Society and Culture* (London: Sage Publications, 1977), pp. 31–35.

2.   Stanley W. Rothstein, "Symbolic Violence: The Disappearance of the Individual in Marxist Thought," *Interchange: A Quarterly Review of Education* 22 (1991): 28–42.

3.   Alfred Schutz, *Collected Papers: Volume 1* (The Hague: Martinus Nijhoff, 1962), pp. 45–49; Alexandre Kojeve, "Lacan and the Discourse of the Other," in *Speech and Language in Psychoanalysis*, trans. Anthony Wilden. (Baltimore and London: Johns Hopkins University Press, 1989), pp. 192–96.

4.   Steven Smith, *Reading Althusser: An Essay on Structural Marxism* (Ithaca, N.Y.: Cornell University Press, 1984), pp. 106–8; Lacan, *Speech and Language in Psychoanalysis*, pp. 290–91.

5.   Pierre Bourdieu, *The Inheritors: French Students and Their Relation to Culture* (Chicago, Ill.: University of Chicago Press, 1979), pp. 1–28.

6.   Herbert Gintis and Samuel Bowles, *Schooling in Capitalist America* (New York: Basic Books, 1976), pp. 53–55; Ira Katznelson and Margaret Weir, *Schooling*

for All: Class, Race, and the Decline of the Democratic Ideal (New York: Basic Books, 1985), pp. 20–22, 46–51; Stanley W. Rothstein, "Schooling in Mass Society," *Urban Education* 22 (October 1987): 267–85.

7. Stanley W. Rothstein, "The Sociology of Schooling: Selection, Socialization and Control in Urban Education," *Urban Education* 21 (October 1986): 295–315; Willard Waller, *The Sociology of Teaching* (New York: Russell & Russell, 1961), pp. 154–59; Willard Waller, "What Teaching Does to Teachers," in *Identity and Anxiety*, ed. Maurice Stein, Arthur Vidich, and David M. White (New York: Free Press), pp. 332–34.

8. Katznelson and Weir, *Schooling for All* pp. 12–13, 16; Bowles and Gintis, *Schooling in Capitalist America*, pp. 21–24, 247–49; David Nasaw, *Schooled to Order*, (New York: Oxford University Press, 1979), pp. 35–37.

9. Waller, *The Sociology of Teaching*, pp. 19–22, 226–29, 232–33, 355; Waller, "What Teaching Does to Teachers," pp. 329–50.

10. Bourdieu and Passeron, *Reproduction in Education, Society and Culture*, pp. 54–67; Basil Bernstein, *The Structuring of Pedagogic Discourse Vol. IV, Class, Codes, and Control* (London: Routledge and Kegan Paul, 1990), pp. 45–46, 134–45.

11. Bourdieu and Passeron, *Reproduction in Education, Society and Culture* pp. 4–7; Stanley W. Rothstein, *The Voice of the Other: Language as Illusion in the Formation of the Self* (Westport, Conn.: Praeger Publishers, 1993), pp. 93–103.

12. Bourdieu, *The Inheritors: French Students and Their Relation to Culture* pp, 3–9.

13. Bourdieu and Passeron, *Reproduction in Education, Society and Culture*, pp. 31–35; Talcott Parsons, "The School Class as a Social System," in *Education, Economy and Society*, eds. Arthur Halsey, John Floud, and Charles Anderson (Glencoe, Ill.: Free Press, 1961), pp. 435–36; Arthur L. Stinchcombe, "Environment: The Cumulation of Effects Is Yet to be Understood," *Harvard Educational Review* 39 (1969): 511–22.

14. Bourdieu, *The Inheritors: French Students and Their Relation to Culture*, pp. 1–28.

15. Bourdieu and Passeron, *Reproduction in Education, Society and Culture*, p. 73.

16. Ibid., pp. 73–74.

17. Ibid., pp. 35–37.

18. Stanley W. Rothstein, "The Ethics of Coercion," *Urban Education* 22 (April 1987): 53–72.

19. Bourdieu and Passeron, *Reproduction in Education, Society and Culture*, pp. 54–67.

20. Emile Durkheim, *Education and Sociology* (New York: Free Press, 1956), pp. 123–26.

21. Peter Blau, *Bureaucracy in Modern Society* (New York: Random House, 1956), pp. 29–30; Charles Washburne, "The Teacher in the Authority System," *Journal of Educational Sociology* 30 (1956): 203–5.

22. Melvin Seeman, *Social Status and Leadership: The Case of the School Executive* (Columbus: Bureau of Educational Research, Ohio State University, 1960); Stanley W. Rothstein, *Identity and Ideology: Sociocultural Theories of Schooling*

(New York: Greenwood Press, 1991), pp. 109–28.

23.   Olive Banks, *The Sociology of Education* (New York: Schocken Books, 1976), pp. 14–22.

24.   Stanley W. Rothstein, "Symbolic Violence: The Disappearance of the Individual in Marxist Thought," *Interchange* 22 (1991): 28–42.

25.   Walter James, *Talks to Teachers on Psychology and to Students on Some of Life's Ideals* (New York: Holt, 1902); Edward B. Leacock, *Teaching and Learning in City Schools* (New York: Basic Books, 1969), pp. 123–25.

26.   Rothstein, *The Voice of the Other: Language as Illusion in the Formation of the Self*, pp. 121–26.

27.   Pierre Bourdieu, "Cultural Reproduction and Social Reproduction," in *Knowledge, Education and Cultural Change*, ed. Robert Brown (London: Taivistock, 1973), pp. 71–72.

28.   Pierre Bourdieu, "The School as a Conservative Force: Scholastic and Cultural Inequalities," in *Contemporary Research in the Sociology of Education*, ed. John Eggleston (London: Methuen, 1974), p. 32–33; Durkheim, *Education and Society*, pp. 70–71.

29.   Rothstein, "Schooling in Mass Society," pp. 267–85.

8

The Other Side of Segregation: Ethnographic Glimpses of an Inner City Junior High School

The images of the modern inner city school are familiar in all the ethnographic studies of the past, where their purpose was to illustrate the realities of racial and economic segregation.[1]

These observational studies sought to alert the citizenry of the nation to the disastrous experiences minority and poor children were having in outdated and impersonal state institutions. A steady stream of such studies was published, and, for a while in the 1960s, it seemed that something might be done about these caretaker agencies. If the soul of U.S. citizens momentarily shrank from the sight of these dreaded houses of confinement that seemed to undermine all efforts at education, it soon adopted more familiar responses of national denial and despair.

One such study was of an inner city junior high school situated in the South Bronx of New York, a poor and segregated community near Yankee Stadium.[2] This school was very much the detention center that its stark architectural design suggested, surrounding itself with high metal fences and windows covered by steel gratings. Many bars, cast-iron doors, fences, locked entrances and exits, flourescent lighting, and barren uniform classrooms confronted the students and teachers as they prepared to do their work each day.

As for the ethos of this urban junior high school, the story is by now a familiar one: the decision to place students from seven surrounding junior high schools at Urbanaire meant that its first pupils were the rejects and malcontents from all over the South Bronx. Those visiting the school to find out whether they wished to teach there were often confronted by wild scenes of student disorder and violence. The principal courteously went out to meet each new batch of inexperienced teachers, while everyone wondered whether the school's reputation was really as bad as the media had portrayed it. The meeting between the embattled principal and the newcomers was a marvel of confusion. Mr. Knott, the principal, immediately began to orient them to their surroundings, cautioning them about the difficulties they might encounter when they began their work in the school. He asked them questions about what they might do in different situations. From most, he received only the banalities and foolish responses of college students who had never taught anywhere, let alone in an inner city junior high school. It was useless to listen to them, he decided. Turning to them in exasperation, he motioned them to stop raising their hands in answer to his repeated questions. "Don't be embarrassed to admit it," Mr. Knott told them moodily. "You don't know what to do. You won't know what to do, at first. You'll feel like things are getting out of control, that you're not going to make it through another day. Don't be ashamed. Everyone feels that way at first. . . . You'll make a lot of mistakes. After all, what do you know about teaching? You've been students all your life!" (Several of the newcomers shifted about uneasily in their seats.) "What should you do?" (Again, hands shot up.) "No, no! Don't raise your hands! Don't think! Just listen! I'll tell you what to do. . . . Pick out one of the experienced teachers on our staff, someone who looks like he knows what he's doing. . . . Then, do what he does. Walk like him. Talk like him. And soon, you'll be like him! Watch the way he gets out of his car each morning, and, then, you do it the same way. Watch how he reacts under pressure, and, then, you do it the same way. Watch the way he controls his students, and, then, you do it in the same way. Before you know it, the words will become your words, the actions will become your actions, and you'll be an effective teacher, too."[3]

These are the initial encounters, at least insofar as they happened in this inner city junior high school: the angry arrogance of the principal and his administrators, who passed on to newcomers the educator's perspective as it had developed after more than a year of incredible stress and failure. The terse assurance of the principal, who ignores the newcomers even as he greets them in their initial orientation. Already, new teachers had been assured that the children were monsters to be kept at bay because of the dangers they represented to order and stability in the school.

The principal's speech, which sought to establish the dangers and separateness that existed between teachers and students, was greeted with stunned silence and disbelief. However, beneath the stolid front of these newcomers, there was some break in their self-confidence, as a few coughed uneasily while others sat in stunned silence.

Was the principal serious, or was this some way of jolting them out of their complacency? Imitate the behavior of veteran teachers in order to become successful in inner city classrooms? Could that really work? Could college graduates without any classroom experience plan meaningful lessons for ghetto youth by imitating the speech and behavior of others? Could they win the respect and affection of their students that way?

The truth, as it turned out, was quite different. There was a continuity in attitudes, of course, with administrators setting the tone for newcomers without apprising them of the terrible history of the school.

The arrogance of Knott, who seemed to put into a few words the dangers newcomers would confront once they began their work with inner city youth, also provided new staff with a way of thinking about this inner city junior high school. Henceforth, novices could distinguish between the incorrigible and intransigent students and the educators who confronted them each day. The true dangers for these young men and women were within and without: teachers had to adopt the attitudes and perspectives of defensive staff members while making common cause with them in the face of constant disorder and disarray.

The ghetto school would serve as an instrument for social and educational segregation. It would continue to function as an educational center that sought to reconstruct around public education an environment as much as possible like that of a correctional institution. This was for obvious reasons. The sight of the unruly and disruptive students was for every newcomer the "obvious" cause of the school's problems. It seemed self-evident to anyone who actually worked in the school, which had to control large numbers of recalcitrant and retarded students who had little or no respect for schoolteachers or public education. This was all calculated to keep things as they had been in the past, even though that past had been so unfortunate for teachers and students alike. However, the principal reason for these practices lies elsewhere: it was that education could play no role other than the one it had played in the past, because it was duty-bound to organize public schools into segregated tracks for middle-class and poor families. It was both tradition and common sense, and, to this extent, it controlled the students in the only way it could, counterbalancing their resistance to segregation and regimentation by endless demands and irrelevant pedagogic efforts. Its underlying ethos had much to do with the loss of freedom and opportunity that accompanied urban poor and immigrant children once they were placed under the supervision of those who are not only strangers to them but also incapable of understanding their role in the economic stratification of U.S. society. To encourage the influence of dominant values and perspectives in minority and poor children was considered of great importance, the essence of effective education. In the minds of schoolteachers, student failures were a deeply personal occurrence that left them in an agitated and frustrated condition, but they remained blameless in their own judgment of the situation. Thus, open forms of bigotry were often ignored or simply unrecognized by staff members:

October 11th: Mister Budge asked me into the teachers' lunchroom where we served ourselves on metal trays. During formal teacher orientations, the teacher's cafeteria is crowded with new and old staff members.

We know some of the teachers in the room, but there are many newcomers. We seat ourselves in the rear and are soon joined by some teachers from our floor. One of them is talking to a young man fresh out of college.

"Have you met any of our student clientele? You won't have any trouble with them once you understand that they're an inferior people."

"Inferior?" The young teacher said.

"Don't tell me you haven't noticed. They're an inferior people. Once you accept that fact they're really very easy to deal with. They're like little children. You have to take care of them and not expect too much." The veteran teacher continued to talk this way. I moved to another table. There, too, the talk was about what you could expect once you began to teach inner city youth.

"This isn't a school. It's a zoo. . . . These kids are animals! Animals! And we're their keepers. I took my home-room to assembly last year and lost half of them on the stairway. When I went back to get them, I found them swinging on the banisters like little monkeys. It looked like a zoo."[4]

The principle of legal coercion and force served as a further instrument of social control in this ghetto school. Anxiety and fear appeared as important features of this segregated institution, but the separation between teachers and students was reinforced by the authoritarian classroom environments that sought to reproduce, as much as possible, the working conditions in the adult society. This was done for two reasons. The sight of disruption and disorder in school buildings was for every teacher and parent a cause of sorrow and despair. It was the origin of all those regimenting practices that had been put into place by educators for more than 200 years! Most Americans generally believed that the diverse populations that gathered in public schools required a unifying and controlling message and methodology. The well-behaved children and the malcontents had to be managed at the same time, often in the same moment and in the same classroom. These pedagogic and disciplinary methods were calculated to stop the unrestrained and idle behavior of students and to fix in their minds the ideology and insights of the educational system. The principal reason for controlling the bodily movements of students became evident when visitors saw the disorder of inner city schools like Urbanaire Junior High School. It was that schooling could play various roles in curbing the natural energies of youth because it disciplined their minds and bodies over many years. In everyday lessons, children could be taught to honor and respect the authority relations of the classroom and, later, of the workplace. Schooling could be a constant restraint on the irresponsible attitudes of youth, controlling and counterbalancing antisocial dispositions and behaviors. Its teachings had to reinforce those of the children's earliest years in their families, making them understand that their status and standing in the school and society were the natural outcome of irresistible forces. This restraining capacity was felt by children on a daily basis as teachers used speech and language to place them in the symbolic world of humans.[5] To encourage youngsters to accept the teaching of educators was considered to be of the greatest importance by businessmen and politicians because it assured the continuance of the Republic and its economic system. In the rationalizations of educators, schooling was composed of concrete practices that could not fail to socialize youth into a proper respect for authority and contemporary society. It carried with it what was essential to the proper raising of children in an environment that simulated the realities of the workplace and the commonwealth. It was the one place where the children of the nation came together for long intervals, learning the folklore and knowledge of their forebears. There, in enclosed and quiet classrooms, they could discover their history and develop the habits and opinions that would allow them to function effectively in the higher reaches of learning and earning. Education protected the old relationships in the workplace by its daily routines and authority structures. This made discipline and order more real for students, providing them with an environment that emphasized constant constraint and confinement. In schools, the educational and moral ethos of U.S. traditions were imposed on children who were not so much educated as they were isolated and controlled for much of their teenage years. At the urban junior high school, this moral suasion was a part of everything teachers did, allowing them to judge and condemn students without looking at their own inadequacies. Socioeconomic and racial segregation had very long histories in the United States, as did schooling's penal and military disciplinary code. That code did not attempt to perceive or differentiate good students from malcontents but attempted to place all youngsters within an institutional setting where their presence needed to be constantly explained. Urbanaire constituted for students an oppressive and sometimes confusing place where they were constantly observed and threatened with sanctions.

October 18th: (In the hallway on the first floor)
   "You! Yes you! Over here!"
   "Me?"
   "Let me see your pass."
   "Pass?"
   "Come on, come on. Your pass."
   "Here."
   "This thing isn't a pass. It's no good."
   "Huh?"
   "It isn't signed by a teacher."
   "No?"
   "Let me see your program card."
   "I'm in Mister Brown's class."
   "I don't remember seeing you around. You better come with me."
   "But why?"
   "Because! You don't have a pass. YOU DON'T HAVE A PASS!"

The presence of a detention center and other disciplinary practices was considered of great importance in managing the bodily movements of students. Fear emerged as an essential presence in the inner city junior high school. Already in this encounter, there is no need to identify who is speaking. It would be unthinkable for a student to begin a conversation by addressing teachers as "Hey you! Yes you!" The right to stop and question individuals resided in the role of the teacher. The teacher was the one who was responsible for the order and control procedures and for determining when another person had the right to be present in a particular part of the building.

The constraints established at the junior high school were of great intensity; they had ritualistic roots that allowed any teacher to stop and question any student anywhere in the school building. The central feature of such encounters was always the question of the student's right to be present in a particular location at a particular point in time. Teacher coerciveness was now endowed with a power to police, to apprehend, and to judge in the same moment. It further strained the already fragile relationships between teachers and students. Here, in these overcrowded, mass schools, education could never free itself from the harsh disciplinary tactics of its past. The important person in these kinds of situations would alway be the teacher, and the teacher's mode of behavior would always be that of the coercive inquirer. Student responses to these searches and seizures were usually defensive or apologetic, helping to establish more firmly the relevant status and membership categories in the school.

Another ethnographic account in this ghetto school tells about the way young boys were treated by the dean of discipline, whose mere appearance caused anxiety and panic in many students.

December 1: Toward the end of the day, I was talking to a student when the boy's dean passed my office, in obvious agitation. His face was purple, his fists clenched. I tried to catch his eye, but he avoided my glance. Quickly he moved toward students who were standing in front of his office. Near the boys, the assistant dean stood waiting impatiently.

I walked down to the dean's office to see what was happening. Upset and angry, our dean could be a difficult man, and I wanted to be there in case something happened.

"Up! Hands up!" Spoken with sudden fury, the dean's voice left little doubt about what he wanted. The boys turned quickly and placed their hands against the wall.

"Higher! Higher! . . . get those legs apart!" Hands and legs moved slowly. A crowd began together. Then both deans sprang into action, frisking first one boy and then the next.

For a moment, I stood there amazed. The dean grabbed one of the boys by his neck and slammed the back of his head into the office door. Then I moved between them and forced him to release the boy. "What the hell is this?" I said.

"A frisking, that's what it is," came the answer. "One of these shits is a thief and I'm going to find out who!"

I stayed between the dean and the boys and asked him to step into my office. But he brushed me aside, saying the "old man" had suggested the search. Some teachers hurried to my side and we kept them from completing their police search, their "frisking." The boys stood quietly to one side. I told them to step into the dean's office and told the dean to interview them. Scowling about "bleeding hearts," he slammed the door. I tried to look cool and in control of myself, but my hands were shaking.

Back in my office, one of the girls who had seen the frisking asked me if I had seen the dean "making nothing of those kids." And of course, I had.

Later I spoke to the principal. He told me I should have minded my own business! "A good frisking never hurt anyone! It shows them we mean business here."[7]

In the light of these reports and others, we must reevaluate the meanings assigned to inner city schooling.[8] Education of the minority and poor children, providing access to children from diverse backgrounds, preparing youth so they could take advantage of the economic prosperity of the United States — these are only deceptions. The actual practices were very much like they had always been in the past. The educational system created a custodial track where the horrors of regimentation and penal discipline were recreated without their previous moral justifications. Hope of preparing inner city youth for a better life no longer dominated the thinking of educators inside these mass schools. Educators now demanded that students accept inmate status inside the school asylum. The inner city junior high school punished children by forcing them to attend essentially caretaker institutions. It transformed the personal identities of students into those of quasiprisoners. Making youth aware of their incompetencies and worthlessness in the educational and social hierarchy. It organized these identities by constantly controlling students while making them acutely aware of their inability to do acceptable academic work. By this continuous penal discipline, the students became objects of constant correction, always open to the impositions of adults. The students were to become completely aware of their ignorant and unworthy condition and their inability to take advantage of the opportunities schooling offered them. This institutional identity made students into objects that could be placed in files. The files could be updated by new observations and judgments about the students' progress or lack of it.

We are in a segregated world where teachers again judge boys and girls according to their ability to read, write, speak, and understand the academic language of the schools. Work and constant drill are paramount in the educational treatment as practiced at the inner city school. Within this constant drill and busy work is a power to control and to regularize the thoughts and bodily movements of students. They are forced to pay continuous attention to the demands of the teacher, the textbooks, the workbooks, and so on. Their obligation is to learn, to memorize, to obey, and to try long after reason would suggest that they cease to do so. Regular, routinized schoolwork has the desired effect among students, forcing them to attend to materials that have a rationale outside their own interests and concerns. It is preferred in mass schools because of its ability to control the behavior of large groups of students.

Those youngsters who are the busiest are thought to be the ones who will get into the least amount of trouble while responding best to the disciplinary and pedagogic demands of the impositional teachers. By listening to and heeding the demands of the teacher, students learn the mores and moral understandings of the industrious men and women of the United States. They submit their own idle inclinations and desires to societal and educational demands that are steeped in morality and the reality of the workplace. Hence, busy work is to be commended and practiced with absolute confidence by schoolteachers. All that is individualistic and imaginative in students must be excluded as being impractical to the goals and practices of effective classrooms. The study of what has been deemed valid knowledge by legal authorities and practitioners must be pursued by educators in order to maintain the highest levels of order and control in school buildings. They are the one and only way to reduce the antisocial elements of the students' personalities, the only way to bring them to discover the forms and responsibilities that are required in schools and in the labor market. The different subjects furnish useful current information upon which students can focus as they struggle to master the language and culture of their neighborhood schools. In the mass school, schoolwork is stripped of an meaningful value. It is imposed only as a moral and political demand of the state. It has the effect of severely limiting the liberty and status of young people in order to force them to submit to an organizational order and ethos that is foreign to them. They are forced to take on responsibilities for which they have little training or inclination. The single aim of this educational training is to categorize youngsters in terms of their standing against other students in the educational system with an eye toward weeding out malingerers and malcontents.

Even more powerful a control structure than schoolwork or constant observation is the youngsters' own need to receive social approval from teachers (and other adults). This need for recognition and approval deeply influences the way students respond to their teachers, operating with peculiar force during the teenage years. In times past, the students were vulnerable to teacher observations of a more pervasive nature, but the observations ceased once they were out of the school building. It involved them and their personal selves only during those moments when they were in the classroom and under the direct authority of the teacher. Modern schooling continued these observations, noting findings and test scores and creating an institutional identity for students that was cumulative in nature and, therefore, all the more pervasive. The students cannot change these observational recordings in any way and are often unaware of their existence. Schooling organized an entire ceremonial ritual around these cumulative files, using them to judge students as successes and failures in their schoolwork. At key moments in the students' careers, everyone was forced to pay attention to these observations and test scores, which were used to constantly categorize and place youngsters. Teacher observations could discover any anti-social attitudes or behaviors, any familial problems, or any awkwardness with the language and culture of the school and record these findings for other teachers. The administrators often used these records to justify their student placements, sharing some of their data with concerned parents. The information was gathered over many years and so had the additional force that comes with cumulative files. Rarely did teachers experience any unpleasantness at these parental meetings, because they habitually divorced themselves from what was happening. "Charles has failed himself by not doing his work," they might say, freeing themselves of responsibility for these omissions or for their decision to fail him. This meeting between parents and teachers had ritualistic beginnings, of course. They were held as though they were a dialogue between concerned parties and organized around the work and behavioral records of the student. Forever cast in the role of ignorant and unworthy persons and observed and challenged every time they failed to conform to the rules of classroom life, the students were obliged to see themselves as these persons who were not doing what they should to succeed in school (or later, in the workplace). The world of the school accepts students only when they succumb to the ethos that governs schooling in mass society, only when they surrender their personal identities and accept their institutional role in the system.

Although some discourse occurs between students and teachers outside their common educational experiences, one tenet of the teaching staff's code is to limit such communications lest it seem like they are playing favorites.

Because all students need the attention and approval of the teacher, the teacher must find a way to control these incessant demands for attention. Raised hands and calls for attention must be discouraged, except when they are specifically requested by the teacher.

Just as talk between youngsters is prohibited, so, too, is student participation in the planning of their education. Such exclusions give teachers another reason for keeping their distance from students. It may become necessary to advise them of their retention in grade or failure to achieve some sought-after educational goal. All this formalism in the contacts between students and teachers helps to keep negative stereotypes alive. Two different views of the school develop side by side but are seldom seen or understood by staff members or observers. With few exceptions, the views of teachers are synonymous with the formal organization and the ideas of old-timers who socialized them. The students, on the other hand, must strive to keep some part of their personal identity separate and apart from the impositional and coercive demands of adults.

The separate worlds of teachers and students are one of the important consequences of the bureaucratic structuring of mass schools. Another is the nature of schoolwork in stratified educational institutions that emphasize social and intellectual selection as one of their primary social functions.[9]

In the structuring of pedagogic actions in inner city schools, the emphasis is seldom upon learning alone. The time it takes the learner to absorb and master materials is of even greater importance in determining the success or failure of a student, but to say that students must learn things at appropriate intervals in only a part of the story. There is the problem, in many inner city schools, of presenting these materials to children in meaningful, sequential fashion. Whatever the official emphasis on learning the elements of the curriculum, the actual focus of teachers is often upon a continuing evaluation that sorts out slow learners and malcontents. There are different tracks waiting for the children of the poor once they have been officially selected and assigned to appropriate classrooms and schools. This is a universal characteristic of schooling in modern society. Individual differences in maturation and cultural backgrounds are ignored in the rush to label students so they may be more easily processed by the institution's communication system.

Often, so little effort is needed to master the work in these segregated schools that students suffer from boredom. Schoolwork is dominated by workbook and textbook activities that turn many students off to learning and the spirit of inquiry. At other times, more than the allotted time is needed before some students can grasp and master the schoolwork, and feelings of inadequacy and failure often accompany these encounters. In some schools for the poor, such as those in the South Bronx, St. Louis, Los Angeles, Boston, and so on, the practice of baby-sitting for students of the urban poor is well-documented. Activities are organized around the school's preoccupation with order and control, and successful academic achievement is rare. In almost all public schools, the students' time and attention are controlled by teachers. The students' sense of importance, their worthiness and competency are damaged by the mechanistic methods teachers employ in their struggle to achieve higher test scores. The following example is also from Urbanaire Junior High School:

November 3: This morning I made my first observation of a veteran teacher. At the front of the room sat Mrs. Harris, the principal's target of the moment. Her large, puffy face was partly covered by tinted spectacles. She seemed edgy and ill-at-ease. Every boy and girl sat silently in their seats. (She must be doing something right! I told myself.) A monitor walked down the aisles distributing materials. To one side, another monitor checked the attendance. A very well disciplined class! Very attentive!

Mrs. Harris gave directions in a stern voice: "Turn to page seventy-four and read page seventy-four through to page eighty-three. Then complete the questions on page eighty-three in your notebooks. Are there any questions? Good. Begin!"

At this command, books were opened and eyes became engrossed in the assigned reading. I was surprised no attempt had been made to motivate the student or to review difficult vocabulary words. They hadn't even speculated about the title or what the story might be about. Still, everyone seemed to be working! Mrs. Harris was working, too. She sat at the front of the room doing clerical chores! I felt confused and deeply troubled. After a few moments, I stood and began to move about the room. Several youngsters had no idea what the story was about. Others didn't know key words or concepts. They scribbled and doodled in their notebooks or just stared out the window.

After twenty minutes or so, everyone was asked to turn back to page seventy-four. Then each student read a paragraph while the others followed along by pointing to the words as they were read aloud. It was just the way they had taught reading in the charity schools of 200 years ago! At that point, I left the room. If this was the way our veteran teachers were teaching, what could we expect from the less experienced members of our staff?[10]

Whether the schoolwork is too easy or too difficult, students who are interested and curious about the world they live in soon lose that curiosity. An example are the poorly taught science lessons in inner city schools that teach "facts" without relating them to the questions, problems, and changing perspectives of modern science.

We see at work in these schools for the poor a suppression of intellectual curiosity and a physical constraint in which the students' selves are placed under constant assault. They are engaged in drill, routines, and standardized classwork under the observation of the teacher, who ceaselessly threatens the students with poor grades and evaluations. Instead of using the needs and concerns of inner city youth to develop a meaningful curriculum and pedagogic style, these segregated schools pursue traditional reward and punishment systems, masking them in an ethos of moral and civic righteousness. Children are ushered into a world of continual judgment at an early age, and teachers learn to use corrective forms of discipline as their forebears did. Student work is judged only by its effect on the order and control of classroom life. Its intentions and needs are ignored in the rush to recreate the social relations existing in schools and society. Education is responsible only for the tangible results it produces. The rest of the pedagogic experience is violated in a world in which teachers rule their classrooms as tiny autocrats. Education no longer exists for the public except when its results are announced (New York City reported in the early 1990s that 75 percent of its African-American students were failing, and California and Texas reported failure rates for Hispanic students at between 41 and 58 percent!)

The separation instituted by schooling the poor in enclosed classrooms and buildings that had bars on their windows and around the property did not encourage community participation. Students experienced only the inspections and scrutinies that moved teachers closer only when they were seeking to understand variances from the norm. Only the values and understandings of this educator stranger were important in the learning situation, and the teacher seemed to always draw back after classroom encounters. The science of educating the poor, as it would develop in the United States, would always be one of social stratification, surveillance, and perceptual judgment. It would never be a discourse between equals.

Already the outlines of a powerful historical tradition of inspection and assessment can be seen running through the entire U.S. educational experience. Lancaster himself laid out the relational structures of these judgmental features of schooling the poor. Horace Mann suggested a similar discipline, talking of the need to prepare youth for their places in the workplace. Something had been born in the nineteenth century and was flowering in the twentieth. Authority had to be maintained at all costs, and the bodily movements and thoughts of students had to be tightly monitored and controlled. Until the end of the nineteenth century, the education of the immigrant and poor was concerned with providing a basic education and keeping youth busy in classrooms and off the streets. Within these goals of assimilation and moral transformation, schools were filled with the failing and the failed of a generation even as they boasted of their few successes. The teachers were often undereducated graduates from normal schools who learned their trade through an apprenticeship that kept things pretty much as they had been in the past. The place reserved by U.S. society for the schooling of the poor was now obsessed with past, forgotten failures and those who were coming to them from lands where different languages and cultures were practiced. The teacher interceded in the normal development of these students to constrain, to observe, to judge, and to use the English language as a challenge and a weapon. The failure to speak and understand English (as it was taught in schools) deprived youngsters of their own language and culture while replacing it with one that rejected them and their families.

THE LANGUAGE OF DEVALUATION

Turning now to students, we can see that regression was easily observable in their classroom behaviors; it was the transference of students' fantasy relations to the new commanding adult and the substitution of behaviors that seemed to work in the past. It was not a real regression in any clinical sense of the that word. Once the students were released from the classroom, they easily recovered their personal identities. Still, classroom behaviors required a reversion to earlier dependent and submissive behaviors so the students could steer through the impositional demands of the pedagogic experience. As infants and children, the youngsters learned many social and linguistic skills, but in schools, they were told to fall back to the passive, silent state of infancy. They were asked to obey the teacher without thought, preparing them for their later roles as the good workers in industrial society.

It is for this reason that teachers mislead themselves when they direct attention to the reality of the pedagogic moment. The rules of classroom life exclude open intercourse between teachers and students, forcing both to playact their roles. The student-teacher apprenticeship sharpens the dichotomy between these two groups and assures their common alienation from one another. The directive leadership of teachers makes it unlikely that they will learn anything substantial about their students' personal identities, needs, and desires. The students under their guidance appear to know less and less as they progress through the school system, showing little willingness to read a book on their own or to study at home. "School's out!" youngsters will tell parents when asked why they never study or read. Thus, the legal and educational efforts of society to school the poor and middle classes end in apparent failure; many students read less and less as they grow older and do less well in schools. They are forced to resist the demands and definitions of teachers, defending themselves as best they can. Teachers control students in classrooms, dividing their authority from state licenses and societal traditions, but they cannot befriend or educate children, they cannot teach them to love learning in such coercive, alienating environments.

Therefore, we can say that the nature of the teacher's work is always focused upon the state curriculum and away from the individual needs of students they "serve." Not only are the words and behavior of students determined by the decisions of the teacher, but, as we have noted, their actions are constantly evaluated and recorded for further assessment and placement. Tracking leads those students who fail in a stigmatized and unrewarding educational experience; millions drop out at an early age, happy to be free of this coercive schooling for the poor. Some teachers do concern themselves with the interpersonal relationships that develop in their classrooms, but these efforts are not supported by educational authorities. In most instances, teachers learn the language and moral understandings of the teaching profession, paying more attention to social control and standardized test scores than to anything else. They fail to grasp how students transfer feelings from past situations, and how teachers develop countertransferences that also confound the relationships that develop in classrooms. Without such insights, teachers can never understand what is happening to them and their students; they can never understand what is behind the behavior of youngsters.

Students use their own words to respond to the flood of words that make up the pedagogy of the poor; they seek to avoid constant corrections and humiliations in front of peers, splitting their identities and becoming students who stifle their inner needs and desires when they are in classrooms. They seem vaguely aware that the pedagogic act is suffused with subjugation and a devaluation of their own competency, self-worth, and personal ancestry and that they are in an apprenticeship training so they can take the places of older workers once they reach adulthood.

In summary, if we remember our history of education in the United States, we have to admit that the schools have organized themselves around arbitrary pedagogic practices and an obsessive concern with student submissiveness and obedience. Progress for students has revolved around meaningless work; the children's natures must be made to accept, without question, this boring work and the social relations of educational production as they exist in state schools. Schooling's arbitrary and authoritarian practices have been in sharp contrast to its ideological pretensions. Its language has divided and separated the classes, defining students according to their race, sex, and ethnicity and making a mockery of equal access and opportunity. Nothing has taught students the ethos of submission more effectively than having to mind the words of their "betters" for such a long training period. It has been in the speech and language of the children that the teacher has found the means and the will to classify them, discerning who they are and who their parents are in the larger social world. Using a command voice, chastising students in front of others, separating them according to their deportment and academic attainments — each of these archaic practices has a part in preparing youth for the authoritarian workplaces awaiting them in the adult world.

PSYCHOANALYTIC PERSPECTIVES

When one uses psychoanalytic perspectives, it becomes clear why schooling is such a traumatic experience for the children of the poor. Pedagogic practices cause students to resist the bureaucracy's definition of them as incompetents and failures. Again, these definitions and judgements of student deportment and achievement are written down in cumulative files that become the children in the eyes of the administrative system, affecting students throughout their educational careers. Verbalization has its own reality, interacting with social constructions in classrooms to present teachers and students with a set of givens they cannot ignore. Through language, the past is remembered and passed on. Teachers react to the words of students, classifying them and separating the good from the bad. They simply attend to their vocabularies and syntax, despising those who are "disadvantaged" and unable to master the academic curriculum. Children find themselves constructed in the language of teachers, coming to see themselves as "bad actors," "remedial cases," or worse, and this is done in constant classroom discourses that permit students' failures to be known to parents and peers and, later, to other teachers. Thus, the cumulative record, containing evidence of previous indiscretions and failures, alerts new teachers to the problems students may present for them.

Pedagogic action is, above all, a spoken representation of the social relations of schools and society, often with discouraging and unpleasant results. Through it, students are subjected to ideological communications that mask the nature of their relations in schools and classrooms. Words fix youngsters in their place, preparing them for a destiny they often are unable to influence. They are seen as students born into meager circumstances or disadvantaged because of their ethnic and racial heritage. Perhaps a more supportive environment would help these rejects to achieve more in their schooling careers, but the competitive, impersonal ethos of state schools causes them to get lost in the shuffle, failing in incredible numbers and dropping out at an early age.

The words that recall the failure of children move between the imaginary and the real world, confounding the behavior of teachers and students alike. Teachers think they know children once they have read the cumulative file or after they have seen them in "action" for a day or two. However, the reality in these instances is only what is real for them and often omits acts of courage and bravery children reveal as they attend impersonal and penallike schools with surprising dignity and grace. Even the hostility of pedagogic practices is ignored by the teacher, because he/she sees his/her impositional actions as helpful ones. The teachers' perceptions are not completely in error, but the language they use tends to separate them from those students who most need guidance and understanding. For the word that structures classroom discourses testifies to the past and, then, in an incomplete and biased way. It is accepted as reality only because the word bears witness to past transgressions, giving them a concreteness they never possessed. Teachers take for granted the restructuring of past events in words without realizing that the words are not the experiences themselves and that teacher provocations and countertransferences are often omitted from these transcriptions. What is more, the time intervals and matura- tion of students are ignored in these educational practices, and young- sters are often forced to begin new classroom experiences with teachers who have been unduly influenced by past records.

So, pedagogic actions use the word and structures created by the word in the past, conferring meaning and intentions to practices that are grounded in ideologies and traditions. Its methods are continuous discourses, during which time the world is made into an intelligible and understandable whole. This is accomplished by forcing a transindi- vidual, imaginary reality onto students, who must either master and internalize it or fail in their academic work. Pedagogic action uses social histories and memories to structure classes and to stratify students. When children enter the state school for the first time, they commit themselves to an institutional identity and training: they agree to play the student role at all times during their life inside the school building. This agreement is supported by state law, which commands students to attend, no matter what their experiences or failures. Now they become the ignorant ones who need instruction; now they become the unformed minds needing adult guidance and molding; now they are the undisciplined ones who must be watched at all times; now they are the childish ones who need to be taught how to work, how to do what they are told without resistances or questions. This student identity is constituted in an intersubjective world in which youngsters must be deferential and submissive to adult mentors who "know what is good for them."

SOCIAL STRUCTURES

It will be seen on reflection that speech and language play a commanding role in the social structures of educational systems. They are the means by which transindividual communications are made possible in classrooms and schools; they are the universal meaning system teachers and students share when they begin work together. Language and the culture it creates are beyond the everyday reality of classroom life, providing teachers and students with ideas and thoughts that make the schooling situation possible.

Speech and language are that part of an educational system's history that is marked by mythology, folklore, and amnesia; they are the proscribed past that has forgotten its own roots and social functions. They can be seen in the huge public buildings that house educational systems — impersonal edifices without character that reveal schooling's structure like inscriptions on forgotten ancient relics and ruins. The language and culture of schooling reveals itself also in the cumulative files and bureaucratic documents in which memories of the past persist, away from the conscious awareness of present-day teachers and students.

Language and the culture it creates in schools can be uncovered in the words and phrases teachers and students use when they speak to one another. The style of life that goes on in school buildings is rooted in understandings that have been passed on from generation to generation and that still have vitality in spite of great changes in student backgrounds and economic progress. The language and culture of schooling can be discerned in the traditions and folklores of U.S. education and in the normative and ethical structures used to validate pedagogic practices; they exist also in the ideologies that, in traditional forms, transform the history of state schools and mask their failure to educate silent armies of immigrant and poor children.

Finally, the language and culture of schooling make themselves known in the contradictions exiting between the goals and outcomes of public schools; they can be found in the distortions made necessary by education's history in modern times and in the discrepancies between schooling's ideological aspirations and the requirements of modern industrial systems. The history of ideas leads to a historization of schooling, a happening that occurred before such thoughts were written down. These carry unintended and unknown messages from forgotten social experiences in the past. This history of education is still another instance of schooling's forgotten past: every historical trauma and success represents a remote page of glory or failure that resonates in the social and educational practices of schools. What has been forgotten about schooling's roots is remembered in its language and daily practices, and these suggest penal and military institutions and a regimenting mentality. The forgotten history of educational systems is the structural reality that teachers and students experience when they enter schools and begin to interact with one another, unaware of the power that people far away from their classrooms wield upon them.

Schooling appears as a given to teachers and students; the buildings and cumulative records cannot be ignored. These affect the motivation and achievement of students and the efforts of teachers. Youngsters may begin their education after a preschooling period during which reading and writing skills were not properly emphasized; they may never have seen a book before and their teeth may ache because they have never seen a dentist. They may find themselves hungry in the morning and during the first hours in school. Their parents may not speak English as their primary language, or they may speak in a way that absolutely classifies them, in the words of George Bernard Shaw, identifying their lower-class position in society. Because these events and understandings are revealed in language, the students may never see how they affect their chances, and teachers may only understand these variables in a superficial way.

The language and culture of schooling, in these circumstances, are an ethos that defines students without their awareness, without their understanding the effects these have on teacher-student discourses and destinies. Often they appear as traditional practices, reflecting the pedagogies developed to deal with problems that occurred in the distant past. These ways of dealing with poor and lower middle-class children have remained intact and seem to have an impetus or life of their own. What schools teach children is the history of social and economic structures they might have lived in if they had lived 30 and more years ago, but this history is presented as a guide to the present; it is presented as facts, not as words that have censored and interpreted past events.

Every experience of failure and rejection in classrooms leaves personal scars. The humiliation of these early student experiences is often repressed and away from conscious retrieval; the successes, when they come, are inflated. However, what has been forgotten still exists and affects the way students and teachers act in present-day classrooms.

When students go through the grade system, schooling's structures seem to have permanence and logic to them that cannot be denied. The world of words that schooling creates has the function of structuring classroom realities into eternal verities. The problems associated with age-segregation practices are seldom discussed, and children move through the system regardless of individual needs or preferences. When they need older students to help them through difficult stages in their development, the older students are often not available. The competitive, class-bound ethos of schooling presents children with a predetermined destiny that is very difficult to overcome.

Teachers are a major factor in these educational practices, in spite of their constant denials. Their training, as we have mentioned, makes it difficult for them to teach children from different cultural and linguistic backgrounds. The profession's practices are steeped in tradition and folklore, not in scientific theory or research. They do teachers little honor and are reflected in the low status and pay teachers receive for their efforts. Passing on the values and beliefs of the state, they transform schools into inculcation centers that transit and validate the power and culture of industrial culture.

NORMATIVE FEATURES OF SCHOOLING

What are the normative features supporting these arbitrary and impositional educational practices? How do they support the modern industrial state? To answer such questions, we must begin with an analysis of civil society's need for tolerable levels of equilibrium and control in the streets, workplaces, and schools; we must recognize the teachers' overriding concern for order and their need to be constantly reassured that they have, in fact, the right to wield power and authority in the classroom. It will be seen on closer consideration that order is necessary if the everyday life of classrooms and civil society is to maintain a tolerable balance, if conflicts are to be held to the minimum.[11] Teachers and business and political leaders face certain political and economic challenges to the order they impose upon others. Their response differs according to the nature and intent of the challenges they face. An analysis of such responses must transcend instrumental conceptualizations of class, language, and rationality. Both civil society and schools have certain assumptions, certain normative suppositions and expectations that are carried over from other civilizations. It is through a dynamic interaction of these linguistic and cultural expectations and normative assumptions that an empirical order is allowed to emerge in classrooms and society: the conflict that develops out of the struggle of individuals and classes to change their present-day economic and social conditions occurs within the context of symbols and ideologies that have been internalized and passed on from one generation to the next.

It is essential to understand the environment within which these conflicts occur before we can grasp their multidimensional nature and our tendency to misinterpret them. The classroom is more than a mere representation or replication of the densely populated urban centers in which economic and social life occurs. In Weber's words, cities include political-territorial aspects as well as economic-market ones. The classroom is the smaller sphere, where these conditions are reproduced along with political-territorial features, although these are most often obscured by the blustering authority of teachers. Everything in classrooms has its corollary in the workplace; although economic-market features in classroom life are subtle and difficult to ascertain, they become more apparent when pedagogic actions are related to sociocultural functions in modern society. Until one looks at the language and culture being disseminated by the schools and contrasts it with the language and culture of students, one cannot understand the class and knowledge stratification functions that schools perform in mass culture.

So, the school must be understood to include the political, economic, and social aspects of civil society. This is important if we are to move aside its ideological effects. The autonomy of educational systems is never more than an apparition, because their primary purpose in society is to reproduce the social relations that exist in schools and in the workplace. Citizens accept schooling because they believe the egalitarian ideologies that support such institutions. They believe that schooling will improve the possibilities for their children, even as statistics indicate otherwise. For educational systems in capitalist society, this ideological effect is important, because the pervasiveness of state bureaucracies allows them to appear as autonomous agencies without parallel in other societies. This appearance of independence is vital to schooling's ideology as an impartial and fair adjudicator of student progress and development, allowing individuals from different classes in society to accept the notion of equal access and preparation for all citizens. However, subjective and communal ties have always bound individuals to their class, their ethnic group, or their political allegiances.

To understand these ties, Weber has challenged us to analyze the normative features supporting the social and educational systems of a particular social formation. For capitalism, the focus seeks to understand the consequences of material change and the uneven distribution of wealth, the religious explanations that inhibit or aid in the development of secular science, and the use of prophecy and nonrational thought in the everyday living experiences of citizens. The cities and schools of previous civilizations created universalistic associations in some instances and failed to do so in others. Weber writes that these associations were fraternal in essence and, often, familial as well. Men and women were either city folk or from the country; the concept of citizen came later and tended to differentiate individuals from both of these types. In modern capitalist society, the concept of urban worker and entrepreneur had a long history in European development and played a commanding role in the development of schooling.

The development of the burgher citizen had profound consequences for the economic structures and distribution systems that preceded the establishment of state schools in the advanced capitalist countries. The results were complicated by the development of the urban proletariat, or worker, concept, which tended to bring together people from different social, economic, and cultural backgrounds. These newcomers were members of no kin groups, save those of their previous native villages. Their cultural remembrances were filled with religious and cult associations and rigid class affiliations. Attempts to organize these urban workers into unions ran into the barriers of their previous understandings and normative values that opposed universalistic associations. Economic classes were formed in capitalist cities and states, composed of burghers who were all deemed to be citizens of equal weight before the law. These citizens were seen as individuals, an abstract legal definition that had no basis in the previous life experiences of rural folk who had migrated to the towns and cities. The tribe or clan or familial relations of the past now were superseded by a less satisfying, less enveloping legal status of citizen. In the state schools, this identity was transformed into students, all of whom were seen to be equal in the eyes of the law, all of whom were given equal opportunities to succeed.

According to Weber, the differences that developed among these citizens were to be traced not to their economic conditions but to their comparative religious understandings and cultural backgrounds. Christianity, as the supreme example, was able to develop a religious community that transcended the relationships of family and class. This was reflected in the schools, where everyone was able to attain the status of student and Christian citizen, regardless of previous status in their countries of origin. Barriers of birth and community were abolished, and all immigrants to the United States, as one example, were given the title of American, for example, citizen. Thus, the power of kinship groups and clans was significantly weakened, and the beliefs of the individual became his/her primary entrée into religious and civil society.

Weber believed that the history of the development of the Western city and state was one of revolution, during which time the lower classes or strata were spurred into action by normative ideals that were peculiarly associated with the burgher ascendancy. This began to occur during the twelfth century, when urban merchants began to have serious conflicts with the aristocratic classes and culture. The rights of citizenship were the normative order used by the new burgher classes to define their rights and privileges in the city and state. The normative changes in perception were accompanied by changes in the material conditions of the burgher class that further encouraged them to participate in the development of civic power that was to become decisive during the next centuries. As with the aristocratic classes, the burghers were separated from the poor of society by their ability and willingness to pay taxes, but their conflict with the nobility developed over their rights as commoners and citizens. A normative egalitarianism developed in these new cities that now spoke of the rights and changes that were needed if trade and commerce were to flow freely. Once the confidence of the burghers reached a certain point, they could no longer tolerate being seen as beneath the lazy, oafish types that predominated in much of the nobility.[12]

Now, educational systems began to reflect the changes in the economic and social distribution structures of the new burgher culture. The urban poor and working classes were won over by ideological promises about freedom, equality, and fraternity, bringing people of the national state together and schooling them in common schools. Of course, the class divisions in society were still reflected in the education and language of individuals and their families, but these were masked by economic associations that seemed less oppressive than those of the feudal period. Attempts to train children in state schools provided nation-states with normative and emotional ties that created patriotic emotions and beliefs. This training produced substitute workers and citizens willing and able to take their places in the economic system as it was. All children were eventually enrolled in these state schools, and children were supposedly evaluated by their academic attainments rather than by their birth into particular families and classes.

The economic, cultural, and religious ties of individuals provided them with starting points in their educational careers; those with economic, cultural, and linguistic advantages soon pulled ahead in the competitive ethos of burgher schools. Nevertheless, all were treated as equals even though the stratification practices weeded out the children of the poorer classes in the elementary grades.

Schools became an important institution in burgher society, as we have seen, taking over many of the socialization and inculcation functions performed by the family and church in precapitalist periods. The rights and privileges of a business society were emphasized by constant discourse in classrooms, along with an affirmation of its ideological and cultural perspectives.

Schooling for the poor was an educational enterprise without education, an enterprise of constant surveillance and judgment and of uniform custody. The last traces of pedagogic orthodoxy had been extinguished long ago. Formerly, the schools for the poor had openly espoused moral suasion and assimilation as their primary goals. Now, inner city schools solely represented the interests of the state and society against the needs of their most disabled youth. The values of the workplace now reigned supreme in these inner city schools, rejecting the attitudes of despair that often suffused the attitudes of the poor.

NOTES

1. Stanley W. Rothstein, "Orientations: First Impressions in an Urban Junior High School," *Urban Education* 14 (April 1979): 91–116; Erving E. Goffman, *Asylums: Essays on the Social Situation of Mental Patients and Other Inmates* (New York: Doubleday-Anchor, 1961); Ray Rist, *The Urban School: A Factory for Failure* (Cambridge, Mass.: The MIT Press, 1973); Charles Bereiter, "Schools Without Education," *Harvard Educational Review* 42 (1972): 390–413; Estelle Fuchs, *Teachers Talk: Views from Inside City Schools* (Garden City, N.Y.: Doubleday, 1969); Harold Garfinkel, *Studies in Ethnomethodology* (Englewood Cliffs, N.J.: Prentice-Hall, 1984); Harold Mehan, *Learning Lessons: Social Organization in the Classroom* (Cambridge, Mass.: Harvard University Press, 1979); Alfred Schutz, *Collected Papers, Volume 1* (The Hague: Martinus Nijhoff, 1962).

2. Stanley W. Rothstein, "Researching the Power Structure: Personalized Power and Institutionalized Charisma in the Principalship," *Interchange: A Journal of Educational Studies* 6 (1975): 41–49.

3. Rothstein, "Orientations," pp. 102–3.

4. Ibid., pp. 98–99.

5. Stanley W. Rothstein, *The Voice of the Other: Language as Illusion in the Formation of the Self* (Westport, Conn.: Praeger Publishers, 1993), pp. 117–23.

6. Stanley W. Rothstein, "The Ethics of Coercion," *Urban Education* 22 (April 1987): 59–60.

7. Ibid., pp. 68–69.

8. Rist, *The Urban School: A Factory for Failure*, pp. 241–44.

9. Talcott Parsons, "An Analytical Approach to Social Stratification," *An American Journal of Sociology* 45 (1960): 841–62.

10. Rothstein, "The Ethics of Coercion," pp. 64–65.

11. Jeffrey C. Alexander, *The Classical Attempt at Theoretical Synthesis: Max Weber* (Berkeley and Los Angeles: University of California Press, 1983), pp. 58–60.

12. Reinhard Bendis, *Max Weber: An Intellectual Portrait* (Garden City, N.Y.: Anchor Books, Doubleday & Company, 1962), pp. 431–35.

9

Language and Pedagogy

Within the impersonal walls of inner city schools where the children of the immigrant and poor are confined, within the classrooms, the detention rooms, and even in the concrete playgrounds, its seems at first glance that adults can act with complete impunity. In these places, teachers use the ideology of education to justify their impositional and disrespectful treatment of inner city students, and the children themselves seem to accept such discipline for their "own benefit." Even though these "lessons" have been taught in U.S. schools for more than two centuries, students and teachers seem unaware of the nature of their work together and unable to make meaningful changes. The overly corrective education of the poor, the constant efforts at moral suasion and thought control, the most insistent demands that students remain immobile and quiet — these are all part of the transformation purposes of state schools. Every bias that education and society possesses, every feeble attempt to assimilate foreigners and the urban poor finds its echoes in the discriminatory methods of public schools. There, the children of the immigrant and poor find failure a constant companion. By a twist of perverted logic, students must maintain a fidelity to an academic language and culture that is foreign to them and cannot be taught effectively by schoolteachers. A difficult task is imposed upon the children of the poor and their teachers: they must work together on materials that neither of them have chosen; they must encourage the unequal competition among students of every class and background even after reason would have urged them to cease such comparisons.

However, this is only the obvious part of schooling's alienating effects: the actions and opinions of teachers are, as a rule, enough to maintain the web of affiliations that ensnares students in the culture of the classroom. Beyond the everyday work in classrooms, there exists the "unintended" learnings of dominance and student submission that are not in the official state curriculum. The words spoken by teachers, the formal lessons and plans, once we remove their ideological veneer, establish nothing but the supreme power of educators and the rejection of all liberty and equality in the classroom. Uncontrolled and incessant teacher dialogue provides students with value judgments about themselves, their families, their cultural histories, their primary languages, their race and sex. Such discourses also evaluate the students' progress through the grade system, providing them with realistic expectations for further education and success in the workplace. The relationship between the teacher and student is made more difficult by the adult's speech and language and the educational and social goals he/she seeks to achieve. Following the logical conclusions of mass institutions and the pedagogy of the poor, the teacher presents the state-validated view of the world, performing pedagogic acts that confuse and trouble students from diverse racial, ethnic, and linguistic backgrounds. The teacher takes their passivity for ignorance, their anger and aggressiveness for a personal assault on his/her efforts and authority.

Here, then, is the source of the regression that others have noticed in such situations.[1] As teachers expand their presence in classrooms, students draw back and revert to ever more infantile behaviors. However, these regressions are not pathological in the clinical sense. They are more an attempt by youngsters to find safety in the dependent behaviors of an earlier period when parents also dominated their every movement and thought. Their present relations with teachers and peers are so disturbing that they must either accept institutional definitions of themselves, withdraw into themselves, or lash out at the offending parties.

So, the everyday educational experiences of teachers and students can be very misleading for them; the effects of words may be understood, but the emotional force behind them may be hidden from view. The rules of classroom life exclude real contact between teachers and students, forcing both to attend to the pedagogic work of the state that only separates them further. Teachers who believe otherwise might retrace their own experiences as students and student-teachers. Seldom, if ever, were they able to contact the real situation or relationship developing between them and their mentors. Perhaps they will remember that the reality of school life or their role as the paid agents of the state was never dealt with, either. The teachers or supervisors performed their work by constant surveillance and by judging students in a competitive ethos. They supervised every movement in the rooms, searching to discover whether students were doing their work in the prescribed manner. The student-teachers or teachers who search their memory may remember, too, how they withdrew their emotions and personal identity from the learning situation, how they deemphasized schoolwork so they could overcome the more impersonal institutional identity of the unknowing and irresponsible student (or student-teacher). In this apprenticeship, teachers learned to teach as they were taught, relying on traditional authority that persists even though legal-rational authority has supplanted traditionalism in mass, bureaucratic schools.[2]

The student or student-teacher acts as a reproductive relay, as do all students, assuring the reproduction and continuity of the social relations of educational production and, through this, those relations that prevail in the social and economic system of adults. Teachers are the ones who first internalize the pedagogic and authority beliefs of the educational system, coming to see things through the eyes of veteran teachers and administrators who preceded them.

Discipline in our present-day schools is still defined by a student's right to be present in a particular place in the school building. An individual's age and place in the organization is the determining factor in deciding who speaks and who listens, who orders and who obeys. Discipline is merely one way that rank is affirmed and strengthened. It designates the authority of adults: they are the ones who assign places to students, routinizing and regimenting schoolwork. Supervision, as we have noted, has become a simple matter of noticing whether youngsters are deviating in some way from the prescribed behaviors and work habits of the teacher.

Paradoxically, this simulation of work environments has had unintended effects. Personal relationships have become so affected by repressed emotions that schools often fail to accomplish their minimal goals. Teaching has become more than a mere recitation and evaluation of rote and arbitrary curriculums; the grading and selecting of successful and unsuccessful children has become an important end in itself. It is necessary to coerce children to be attentive to meaningless work without questioning its efficacy. Observers have been quick to note the consequences: teachers have become little more than drillmasters, preparing children for tests; children have become less human and less involved and more robotized. The schoolwork has become unbearably boring and meaningless to students; their deportment is more suitable for a factory, office, or military camp than an educational institution. Obedience is what has been sought by teachers, yet, it has subverted thinking and inquiry. Students take their places quietly and sit through lessons without involving themselves or being properly prepared.

If teachers could remember their own schooling experiences in these repressive educational systems, they might loosen their control a bit. The greatest advantage they could derive from their situation would be to place themselves in the children's position, imagining their feelings toward the teacher and classroom life. Then, the teachers could begin to deal with some of the reality that lies beneath the formal behavior of students. They might listen to their children's words, understanding that they could learn much from them. If this were to actually happen, questions would surely be raised about what students were leaning and why the lessons were so boring, the discipline so encompassing.

Without this two-way communication, the teachers must fall back on their imaginary relationships with students. They will then be forced to fill in the blanks when children come to school unprepared or late or are absent. Assuming the all-knowing, always-talking teacher role will shut students out of classroom discourses, closing down open communication among them. The teachers will not be able to hear the students' frustrations and confusions; they will not know how their efforts are being experienced by the children they are supposed to serve. They have no other way of learning what is happening in the classroom other than this open, two-way discourse, and such discourse is impossible as long as the teacher is the "boss," the dictator of all decisions made in the room.

Students will speak in empty words when they are called upon to recite in these penallike settings. Their desires, aspirations, hopes, and fears will never come to the surface; they will never commit themselves to classroom experiences that dominate and control them. Their words will have less and less value for them and for their teacher. Too many of the individual psychological factors of the classroom's reality are missing from such encounters. Teachers may believe their role is to modify the individual behavior and character of students, but such actions force children to defend themselves against the hidden message of rejection contained in such communications: you are not good enough as you are — if you were, it would not be necessary to change you.

Discipline in the mass school is a form of power that uses an entire complement of methods, procedures, levels of application, and so on. It is a technology concerned with correction and control, with teaching children by constant discourse who they are and what they can expect in the social and economic world of adults. It is exercised by teachers who are responsible for reintegrating the power and authority of educators during the schooling process.

Discipline is the art of surveillance; under the appearances of classroom decorum, the teacher searches for the uniform behavior and responses of students; behind the demands for standardized responses and learnings, there is the need to train youth who will be useful in capitalist society. The performance of disciplinary actions reinforces the power and status of those who have been legally sanctioned to operate our educational system.

A capitalist society obsessed with punctuality, competition, order, and predictability is a consequence of historical forces that go back several centuries. In schools and other bureaucratic and corporate structures, similar methods are used to insure the continuation of the social status system. This phenomenon of reproduction can be observed in every society of which we have knowledge: every system is confronted with the problem of maintaining and sustaining itself. However, the disciplinary methods of the modern mass school organizes itself in order to achieve five specific functions:

1. to obtain control and power over students by referring to commonly held values and beliefs that are part of the United States' social heritage;
2. to decrease resistance to schooling's decreasing visibility by the use of buildings, classrooms, and detention centers that are partitioned off from the surrounding communities;
3. to bring the effects of their authority and power to its greatest strength by using them throughout the school day;
4. to justify this coercion and control of the student's body and mind by linking such practices to the outcomes of educational agencies; and
5. to increase the usefulness and docility of students so they can perform more effectively in the mechanistic world of work without questioning the power structures they encounter there.

These aims of school discipline coincide with those of business in industry. One consequence of the Industrial Revolution was the enormous rise in the numbers of people on Earth. This population tended to move about more, thereby thwarting the aims of those who sought to keep them in their places so they could be managed and controlled. A change of this magnitude forced legal-rational educational agencies to imitate the disciplinary practices of military, religious, and penal institutions. By the middle of the twentieth century, billions of people were counted in the world's populations. This was also associated with worldwide problems of productivity and economic distribution and the development of bureaucratic systems that train workers not to walk away from the increasingly rationalized, boring work. The development of disciplinary systems is no doubt linked to these new conditions and the rise of bureaucratic authority and society. Legal-rational power was built into the organizational structures of modern institutions so they could vastly increase the productivity and manageability of workers.

From this we conclude that schooling must be understood within a historical context. The life of teachers and students today is the outcome of schooling and economic conditions as they existed at the end of the nineteenth century and earlier. The view of students as ignorant and unworthy persons has its roots in the charity schools of the early 1800s and the reform schools built for Irish truants in 1849. Schools constructed student images that fit their status and class positions in society. However, subjugation was and is the condition of children, even when their educational attainments are high. All students represent a captive, passive audience that cannot speak or move until told to do so. The arbitrary curriculum is not equally understandable or available to students; their race, ethnicity, sex, primary language, and health care all conspire to make the competition of educational knowledge less equal than it appears to be. The relations set up by classroom teachers bind children to an educational effort on their own behalf. They are to seek education and enlightenment, to make something of themselves now and in the future. The contradictions between the ideology of democracy and the realities of their class positions are never analyzed. Public education can be shown to have democratic value only if it can lift working-class and minority children out of their exploited and disadvantaged positions, and this, it has not been able to do. Students are forced to attend neighborhood schools, causing them to learn in racially and economically segregated classrooms. The contradictions of such schooling have their causes in the demands of state schools and pedagogues and the differences between the language and culture of students and academia. The effects of class positions play themselves out in the number of children who eventually attend the best colleges, medical schools, and so on and those who must settle for the lesser schools and occupations in mass society. The reception of the official pedagogy of state schools varies with the differences that exist between them and those of the students they teach.

The students have an existence only in their school; they are constructed by the educational discourses of adults and forced to accept them. These have an ideological component to them but are played out in the daily give-and-take of classroom life. The real world is only what is real for teachers and students working together in enclosed classrooms. The history and state laws and policies structuring pedagogic work are beyond the knowledge and understandings of most teachers and students.

From these observations we can see that it is impossible for state schools to incorporate active, inquiring behavior from students. Their rationale is corrective, coercive, and oriented toward inculcation and reproduction. They are antidemocratic in history and practice, stripping students of inalienable rights to move or speak freely. Linguistic productions and the social structures they created in the past interact in the present, affecting the kind of social relations that develop in classrooms and workplaces. Schools show no interest in working-class children, preferring to treat children as classless persons: they are all students. Until the integration movement forced race into the national consciousness, state schools were comfortable with segregation, as they are in today's resegregated school system. They are aware of the poorer classes only when they fail or drop out of school. Otherwise, the minority, the poor, and the females are shadowy faces performing standardized educational tasks in penallike, impersonal classrooms. There is an imaginary conception of public schools that treats all children as equals with equal opportunities to achieve academic success, and this ideological effect persists in spite of mountains of evidence to the contrary. If educational systems really were interested in preparing youth for their lives as citizens in a democratic society, they would have to analyze and rethink their own practices and social functions. This is not something schools have the power to do, because the licensing, funding, and operation of educational systems are state matters. Schools are condemned to reproduce themselves and the society no matter how harmful such efforts may be for the educational and psychological well-being in children.

However, the passive reception of the arbitrary curriculum and practice of state schools is only the tip of the observable iceberg. These structures were conceived in language; they have survived long after they were developed to solve problems in our nation's past. The methods used to regiment and assimilate immigrants from Europe during the nineteenth century are still being used as the twentieth century comes to a close. Class size, which was always a problem, is sneaking up to 40 children in classrooms in many areas of the United States. These practices are legitimized by the ideological understandings; they are internalized by the word presentations and social structures that fix them in the shared symbolic order of all citizens. Educational practices are seldom seen as historical products, the result of the system's need to reproduce itself. They are seldom related to the Lancastrian schools for pauper boys or the need to recreate the labor power of the future in a commodity-producing and consuming society. However, within all of these deterministic forces, there are rare evidences of free will and an active pursuit of academic knowledge and success. These are exceptions, of course; the silent armies of immigrant and poor children experience schooling as a succession of traumas and failures. The cultural product of schooling is tied to its social functions, attracting support because of the system's demand that children be prepared to assume duties as adults in a grossly unequal society. Students are given the opportunity and an imaginary order emphasizing the "hope" that they will succeed. There is an obvious and unending tension between the words that describe classroom life and the reality. That reality insists upon a complete transformation of the self of students; in many instances, children must give up their culture and language, and in many others, their sex or race is demeaned. The degradation and humiliations of constant passivity and submission lead to a certain type of student and citizen, able to take a place in the classroom or workplace without questioning the social relations that exist there.

The first thing that becomes clear to anyone studying classroom life is that a struggle for dominance and power exists between teachers and students. Conflicts are ongoing, persistent, and less onerous than those occurring in the workplace. Yet, the dominance-submission relationship of the classroom has its roots in the precapitalist period and earlier, when the master-slave role set was more easily visible.[3]

Children repress their social needs and desires in the classroom because they have accepted the imaginary ideas (or ideologies) of education: schooling is a serious and important enterprise deserving attendance and respect. Students accept their subordinacy and regimentation because all of their own kith and kin have advised them to do so and because of their own dependent status in their family and communal relations. Yet, on another level, there is unconscious conflict and struggle for supremacy between teachers and students, and teachers are quite aware of it.[4] Children can never accept their institutional identities and the negation of their personal selves; they must, on some level, always struggle against the conscious and reasonable arguments of adults. Relationships in the cultural order may speak about unified efforts to achieve common goals, but the reality of the struggle for dominance in classrooms is a constant negation of such ideological pronouncements. Teachers use speech and language in their attempts to exercise control over students, while youngsters defend themselves as best they can. The danger point may occur when immigrant and poor children decide they have nothing to gain by integrating themselves into the coercive educational environments of mass schools; without the consent of students, no pedagogic situations can be constructed by educators. Teachers have the decisional rights over students, but only as long as children are willing to concede them these rights.

The ability to force youngsters to move on command and do schoolwork is only too well-documented in the educational literature, but its psychological and educational consequences are universally ignored. Children are filled with ambivalence toward their adult mentors; they have repressed animosities that are often hidden from teachers. (Any rights they may have had to control their bodily movements and thoughts are given up once they enter the school.) However, they sense that the teacher's authority rests on a fragile social compact and that such agreements can come apart. As long as students accept schooling as a legitimate and worthwhile activity and renounce their own desires and needs, the authority of teachers is secure, but when years of failure diminish the children's acceptance of the pedagogic discipline, youngsters usually act up and drop out.

Until this happens, schoolwork follows the dictates and intentions of teachers, further alienating students from themselves and their education. Not only is the learning dictated by the teacher — mimicking the dominance-submission relationships of traditional schools and workplaces — but the students' achievements are short-term and often meaningless to them. They cannot see themselves or their life experiences in the pedagogic efforts of state schools. They wait for passage through the grade system to end so they can begin to live their lives again. However, they also identify with teachers in an ambivalent way and, as a result, are often cajoled into accepting the negative roles of their educational identities.

Still, students seek to deceive their taskmasters by feigning interest while doing as little as possible to get by. Here the ego seeks to silence the demands of the superego as best it can. To gain favor with the mercurial, all-powerful pedagogue, the pupils perform their schoolwork and submit to the constant evaluation and correction of their thoughts and movements. It is their way of partially disarming their tormentor.

From the moment classroom work begins, both teachers and students seek to defuse the fears and anxieties of the other, and students never tire of assuring teachers that they are harmless and pose no threat to the teachers' power and authority.

It is not surprising, then, that many teachers speak disdainfully of students when they are alone with one another. They disparage their educational achievements, even when these are on or above grade level. Their severest barbs are reserved for those millions of inner city and minority children from different cultural and linguistic backgrounds. The children's resistance and response to these attitudes can be observed in their failure to do anything more than what is absolutely required of them.

Here we are at the hub of the controversy Waller spoke about many years ago. In the struggle to force youngsters to learn mandated curriculums, language, and social status, the seeds of constant conflict are sown. If teachers would allow children to learn what was of interest to them, very little conflict would take place in public school classrooms. The word would then be used to explore the complexities of the students' world, and their personal identities could be preserved. However, because this cannot be in state schools, there is nothing but resistance and repression, even in the segregated, suburban schools. Does this mean that educational systems are failing in their mission? Of course not; they achieve their functions of inculcation even if teachers are unaware of what they are actually doing in classrooms. They prepare youth to adapt to the boss-worker dichotomy of the workplace by forcing youngsters to accept the unequal relationships that exist in state schools and classrooms.

Pedagogic action achieves its effects in the social and cultural structures it creates in the minds of teachers and students. These lie at the center of the social identities developed in schooling and, later, in the labor market. Such identities are institutional ones, structured in negativity though a tradition of unconscious understandings that predate the modern period. They permit teachers and students to recognize one another while misrecognizing the true nature of their socially constructed classroom situations. In the beginning, there are open resistances; the children seek to return to their personal identities and familial associations in a nostalgia for the nurturing environment. Later, they come to accept their student identity and the others in the classroom, but this often takes time. Now the student finds that he/she is one of many, competing for recognition in an impersonal, standardized setting. The students transfer emotions and understandings from their pasts onto their teachers and playmates and are unaware of the counter-transference that often occurs. It is only in the early primary grades that the full force of schooling's effects begin to be felt as a negative, rejecting, and unsatisfying experience.

The students in these early grades have a desire to be recognized as separate, unique persons. They seek recognition, not as a group member, but as an individual. They seek to rediscover themselves in the group activities of pedagogy and withdraw once they become frustrated and confused by classroom practices. They become conscious of themselves through the recognition they receive from teachers and students. They learn that their consciousness is really self-consciousness and that this exists within themselves. It is merely a reflection transmitted in language and their own imaginary order. They can exist only if the teacher recognizes them in a dialectic of dominance and submission, if the teacher permits them to stand, get out of their seat, or speak.

Words designate things in the classroom world, allowing teachers and students to see the environment as a self-evident and unchangeable given. In pedagogic actions, the transference occurs through the person of the dominant adult because he/she has the actual power and authority in the classroom. The teacher interprets the students' words and behavior by constantly evaluating and grading them.

When we speak of the relations between teachers and students, we have in mind one thing: the power and authority that teachers have over every movement and thought of children in schools. We cannot put it any other way. These outcomes of pedagogic action lead to the ideological controls and violence that European scholars have spoken about and to serious misrecognitions of the schooling situation by participants. Teachers routinely refuse to acknowledge the role they play in the failures and frustrations of their students; they do not want to face their complicity in the poorly schooled and drop-out students whom educational authorities have labeled as failures. They use language and culture to stratify knowledge and the speech and backgrounds of students to stratify the children themselves. They use the printed word to deny school failures the opportunity to progress further in education or to vie for the more important and desirable jobs in the labor market. The grading practices of teachers unite and divide teachers and students in the same moment; students need the good will of teachers if they are to make progress through the system, even as pedagogues tend to destroy open communications and the educational experience. Students come to mistrust teachers even as they need recognition and acceptance from them. Teachers use the grading power to control the behavior of their charges even as they seek their love and acceptance.

To sum up: repressive student defenses are a natural consequence of the attack on the self accompanying pedagogic actions in state schools. The children have the experiences of the oedipal adjustment to guide them as they deal with this new, powerful adult and the threat the teacher poses to their normal desires and need for recognition. Students may want to strike out at the teacher in order to be rid of him/her and the onerous experience of schooling, much as they wished their fathers out of the way or dead, and so on. They must protect themselves; they must defend against the daily humiliations of classroom life. They must do this while trying to fit into the pedagogic system and social controls of educational authorities. They cannot reject their educational experiences without drawing upon themselves the opprobrium of parents and teachers. They cannot condemn pedagogic practices, because they are supported by the myths, traditions, and ideologies of modern capitalist states. They cannot disavow education (they do not want to learn what every adult tells them they should learn, their parents will be disgraced if they fail or drop out of school, and so on). Their withdrawal from the educational system would simply validate schooling's mandate and function in mass society: sort out and stratify students so they can be prepared for places in the educational and socioeconomic pyramid.

As regards the reasons for the children's attendance, one needs only to consult the compulsory attendance laws and the demands and acquiescense of parents and other "good folk." The children are used to free movement and a reasonably open expression of aggressive and sexual feelings in the home environment. Before they enter school, they have learned to differentiate themselves from others; they have become a "me" who exists as a separate person and an "I" who acts upon the environment to achieve desires. However, once the children enter the state school, the teacher appears as the one who has the right and duty to control their bodily movements and gestures; the teacher is the one who can force them to "sit still" and "be silent"; the teacher can punish and humiliate them with a word when they act out aggressive or sexual feelings. The student is still a "me" in the classroom; he/she can still be referred to as an individual member of the classroom group. However, he/she is extremely limited in the amount of time he/she can act as an "I," changing the classroom environment to suit his/her own needs and desires. The teacher now takes the place of the parent, even when unaware of what is happening. This substitution differs from the real parents of the child because of obvious biological reasons and because the teacher functions only during the school day.

The teacher is related to the students by a dialectic of dominance and submission, aggressiveness and passivity. The teacher is the only important signifier in the room, the only one who can say what is to be done or what is being done in his/her domain. The teacher is a singular presence who commands the attention of the students while recognizing them only in their institutional roles. Education derives its power from these coercive practices and from the students' willingness to accept and internalize them: they are for the students' "own good." The language relationship between teachers and students, with no interlocutor between them, almost always results in one-sided discourses and evaluations. The teachers tell their charges what the learning situation is and why they are ethically bound to force the children to attend to it. By the very fact of the teachers' singularity, by their constant talking and commanding, they impose their will through continuous discourse.

Even if the work is meaningless for the students, even if they are powerless to change their condition in the classroom, they may not say what is on their minds; they may not say what they mean. Thus, the relations between teachers and students are established through a series of closed communications. The students seek to turn the teachers into substitute parents through a transference of previous thoughts, feelings, and behaviors. They give these new dominant adults the attributes of others whom they have known in the past. Unconsciously, they substitute these older images for the teachers who stand before them, determining their behavior by reenacting actions and attitudes that worked well for them in these previous relationships. While this is happening, the teachers are also using countertransference to govern their reactions to students. Their relations are individual to individual, even though the students' behaviors are always seen as being part of a group phenomenon. Students cannot recognize these unconscious defenses they erect, and teachers are often unable to take the place of the other and understand how the children really feel about things. Teachers are also unaware of their prejudices toward children from different social and ethnic backgrounds, preferring to believe that "they treat all of their children the same."

There can be no doubt that the teacher-pupil relationship is an unconscious one, molded in constant discourse and a cumulative written file; both engage in classroom interaction without being aware of the power of others who are not in the room or who lived long ago. This misrecognition of the political sources of their behavior is compounded by the work that goes on between them, work that is determined by the political and social order they share and the educational structures that were created in the past and now act on them as though they were independent, immutable forces. From the beginning, teachers and students learn to perceive and internalize their relationships by referring to others who may not be in the situation. These powerful social identifications mark students and teachers alike, but it is with the students from poor families that the school's inculcation function is most concerned.

Finally, the development of the students' institutional identities is a central feature in the formation of their class position in capitalist society. Schooling is a centering, limiting experience for children, one that tames their animal natures and prepares them to accept a life of labor. The central feature of schooling is one of communication; the linguistic and cultural order creates a world of words permitting participants to make sense of classroom life. Language, as we have noted earlier, is an intersubjective phenomenon, separate and apart from those individuals who use it to speak and communicate. It is something known and available to teachers and students, in the most favorable situations; it acquires a social dimension when the mimetic structures created by the language of individuals in the past also interact with teachers and students, presenting themselves as social realities that exist apart from the will of present-day persons. Thus, the many-sided relationships between signifier and signified are complicated by ideological apparatuses that the state uses to protect its interests.

The world of language and ideas is different from the traditional schooling structures that exist today. Commonsense meanings of words mask the intentions that precede all speech; the ambiguity of communications is eased by the imagination, of course, and by clarifying statements that seek to grasp the meaning of the real world. The social structures of society can be seen as those forces that determine where and how schooling the poor will take place, while the speech and behavior of participants represent attempts to exert their free will within the limited horizons of state schools.

Since the end of the nineteenth century, schooling the poor has been characterized by disciplinary structures associated with massive, bureaucratic institutions. These have condemned new generations of immigrant and poor children to a schooling experience obsessed with selection, confinement, and discipline. Whether immigrants have been from Europe or South America or Asia, they have found themselves beset by powerful indigenous forces that demanded assimilation and the renunciation of their languages and cultural heritages. In spite of calls for more humane and scientifically validated pedagogic actions, schooling has remained tradition bound and unchanging. We are in the habit of subjecting the children of the poor to public humiliation on a daily basis, righteously, and without thinking deeply about the effects such traumatic handling have on all the youth of our nation. We end this book with a warning to schoolteachers and a quote from the Jewish Talmud that seems relevant:

WHOEVER HUMILIATES SOMEONE IN FRONT OF OTHERS IS TO BE CONSIDERED AS ONE WHO HAS KILLED HIM.

NOTES

1.   Sigmund Freud, *Introductory Lectures on Psychoanalysis* (New York: W. W. Norton, 1977), pp. 21–22, 295–97.

2.   S. Clarke, V. J. Seidler, K. McDonnell, K. Robins, and T. Lovell, *One Dimensional Marxism: Althusser and the Politics of Culture* (London and New York: Allison and Busby, 1980), pp. 204–7.

3.   Jacques Lacan, *The Seminar of Jacques Lacan: Book II: The Ego in Freud's Theory and in the Technique of Psychoanalysis 1954–1955* (New York and London: W. W. Norton, 1991), pp. 20–21.

4.   Willard Waller, *The Sociology of Teaching* (New York: Russell & Russell, 1932); see also Richard Altenbaugh, *The Teacher's Voice* (London: Falmer Press, 1991) for the best example of this process.

Selected Bibliography

Berger, Peter and Luckman, Theodore. *The Social Construction of Reality*. New York: Penguin Edition, 1971.

Berthoff, Robert. *An Unsettled People: Social Order and Disorder in American History*. New York: Harper & Row, 1971.

Bourdieu, Pierre. *The Inheritors: French Students and Their Relation to Culture*. Chicago, Ill.: University of Chicago Press, 1979.

Bowles, Samuel and Gintis, Herbert. *Schooling in Capitalist America*. New York: Basic Books, 1976.

Cremin, Lawrence A. *The Transformation of the School: Progressivism in American Education*. New York: Random House, Vintage Books, 1964.

Cubberley, Ellwood P. *The History of Education*. Cambridge, Mass.: Houghton-Mifflin, 1920.

Dewey, John. *Experience and Education*. New York: Macmillan, 1938.

Durkheim, Emile. *Education and Sociology*. Glencoe, Ill.: Free Press, 1956.

Foucault, Michel. *Discipline and Punishment: The Birth of the Prison*. New York: Pantheon Books, 1977.

Fuchs, Estelle. *Teachers Talk: Views from Inside City Schools*. Garden City, N.Y.: Doubleday, 1969.

Greer, Colin. *The Great School Legend*. New York: Basic Books, 1972.

Hummel, Robert C. and Nagle, John M. *Urban Education in America*. New York: Oxford University Press, 1973.

Kaestle, Carl E. and Vonovskis, Maris A. *Education and Social Change in Nineteenth Century Massachusetts*. Cambridge, Mass.: Cambridge University Press, 1980.

Katz, Michael B. *The Irony of School Reform*. Cambridge, Mass.: Harvard University Press, 1968.

Katz, Michael B. *School Reform: Past and Present.* Boston, Mass.: Little, Brown, 1971.

Katz, Michael B. *Education in American History.* New York: Praeger Publishers, 1973.

Katz, Michael B. *A History of Compulsory Education Laws.* Bloomington, Ind.: Phi Delta Kappa Educational Foundation, 1976.

Katznelson, Ira and Weir, Margaret. *Schooling for All: Class, Race, and the Decline of the Democratic Ideal.* New York: Basic Books, 1985.

Lewis, David W. *From Newgate to Dannemora: The Rise of the Penitentiary in New York 1796–1848.* Ithaca, N.Y.: Cornell University Press, 1965.

Nasaw, David. *Schooled to Order.* New York: Oxford University Press, 1979.

Parsons, Talcott (ed.). *Theory of Social and Economic Organization.* New York: Oxford University Press, 1947.

Ravitch, Diane. *The Great School Wars: New York City 1805–1973.* New York: Basic Books, 1974.

Rice, Joseph M. *The Public School System of the United States.* New York: Century, 1893.

Rothstein, Stanley W. *Identity and Ideology: Sociocultural Theories of Schooling.* New York: Greenwood Press, 1991.

Rothstein, Stanley W. *The Voice of the Other: Language as Illusion in the Formation of the Self.* Westport, Conn.: Praeger Publishers, 1993.

Trollope, Franklin. *Domestic Manners of Americans.* New York: Knopf, 1949.

Tyack, David B. *Turning Points in American History.* Waltham, Mass.: Blaisdell Publishing, 1967.

Tyack, David. *The One Best System: A History of American Urban Education.* Cambridge, Mass.: Harvard University Press, 1974.

Waller, Willard. *The Sociology of Teaching.* New York: Russell & Russell, 1932.

Index

ABOUT THE AUTHOR

STANLEY WILLIAM ROTHSTEIN is Professor of Education and Social Foundations at California State University, Fullerton. He is the author of *Identity and Ideology* (Greenwood, 1991), *The Voice of the Other* (Praeger, 1992), and *Handbook of Schooling in Urban America* (Greenwood, 1993).